P9-DGW-820

FINDING a CAREER

Careers If You Like the Arts

Stuart A. Kallen

ReferencePoint Press®

San Diego, CA

About the Author

Stuart A. Kallen is the author of more than 350 nonfiction books for children and young adults. He has written on topics ranging from the theory of relativity to the art of electronic dance music. In addition, Kallen has written award-winning children's videos and television scripts. In his spare time he is a singer, songwriter, and guitarist in San Diego.

Picture Credits

Cover: iStockphoto.com
 9: Depositphotos/scyther5
45: Depositphotos/elvinstar
61: Shutterstock.com/Miriam Doerr

© 2017 ReferencePoint Press, Inc.
Printed in the United States

For more information, contact:
ReferencePoint Press, Inc.
PO Box 27779
San Diego, CA 92198
www.ReferencePointPress.com

LIBRARY OF CONGRESS CATALOGING-IN-PUBLICATION DATA

Names: Kallen, Stuart A., 1955- author.
Title: Careers if you like the arts / by Stuart A. Kallen.
Description: San Diego, CA : ReferencePoint Press, Inc., 2017. | Series: Finding a career series | Includes bibliographical references and index.
Identifiers: LCCN 2016022853 (print) | LCCN 2016024551 (ebook) | ISBN 9781682820087 (hardback) | ISBN 9781682820094 (eBook)
Subjects: LCSH: Art--Vocational guidance--Juvenile literature. | Design--Vocational guidance--Juvenile literature.
Classification: LCC N8350 .K35 2017 (print) | LCC N8350 (ebook) | DDC 700.23--dc23
LC record available at https://lccn.loc.gov/2016022853

CONTENTS

Introduction: Real Solutions for
Everyday Lives   4

Graphic Designer   7

Multimedia Artist and Animator   16

Fashion Designer   25

Photographer   33

Landscape Designer   42

Production Designer   51

Music Therapist   59

Game Designer   67

Interview with a Landscape Designer   75

Other Careers If You Like the Arts   78

Index   79

Introduction: Real Solutions for Everyday Lives

If you have an eye for art, an ear for music, a flair for design, or a passion for fashion you can use your talents to pursue a career in the arts. The arts emphasize imagination, creative problem solving, a willingness to experiment, and the courage to seek new paths while ignoring the status quo. These qualities are attractive to employers in a wide variety of fields. The arts are also seen as a necessary element for businesses to remain competitive in the United States, as a 2013 resolution passed by the House of Representatives notes: "Art and design provide real solutions for our everyday lives, distinguish United States products in a global marketplace, and create opportunity for economic growth."

Students who major in the arts—theater, graphic design, music, animation, fashion, photography—are able to follow their muse and exercise their imaginations every day on the job. And some who were driven by their love of the arts have used their aesthetics to impact society and culture. Industrial designer Jonathan Ive designed the iPad, iPhone, iWatch, and other Apple products which fundamentally changed the look and feel of digital devices. The name of fashion designer Ralph Lauren is seen on jeans, shirts, and other clothing sold throughout the world. Photographer Annie Leibovitz makes her living taking portraits of the world's biggest celebrities. And animator Matt Groening created *The Simpsons*, the longest running primetime TV show in history, which has earned him half a billion dollars.

Freelance Opportunities

While the world of art and design is populated by superstars, most people who work as designers, fashionistas, photographers, and animators will never be rich and famous. In fact, according to the Bureau of Labor Statistics (BLS), employment in most artistic fields is predicted to grow at only 2 percent through 2024. That is slower than the average of 7 percent for all occupations. But the jobs will still be there; by 2024 nearly eight hundred thousand people are expected to be working in art and design occupations. Major growth is expected in fields that provide animation and visual effects for video games, movies, television, and smartphones. And art and design workers will be in demand to create attractive and effective websites and other media platforms.

There is another aspect to careers in the arts that BLS statistics do not address. As demand for highly skilled, specialized employees increases more businesses are hiring freelancers—people who work for themselves. This is backed by a survey from the Freelancers Union and Upwork which shows that about one-third of all Americans worked freelance jobs in 2015. Of that group, 50 percent said they would not quit freelancing and take a traditional job with an employer—no matter how much it paid.

People trained in the arts can find work in some of the top industries that hire freelancers, including publishing, graphic design, web development, entertainment, health care, clothing production, and advertising. Companies that hire the most freelance artists and designers include GoPro, Bloomberg, US-Reports, and Nintendo.

For someone just starting out in the work world freelancing can seem like a dream; no demanding bosses, obnoxious coworkers, inflexible schedules, or long commutes during rush hour. But as anyone who runs a freelance business will tell you, it's not an easy way to make a living. Freelancers have to be extremely self-motivated to work alone and finish projects on time. And, as freelance designer Lance Padgett notes on the Rasmussen College School of Design website: "Creativity and design skills are only half the battle." Freelancers also need to be skilled in accounting, client relations, entrepreneurship, marketing, and project management.

Benefits and Rewards

Of course, not all artists and designers work for themselves. And people with a knack for art, music, and design can find traditional job opportunities at companies that offer great benefits and work settings. Multimedia artists and animators can work at renowned Hollywood studios with the top talent in the entertainment industry. Video game designers are employed by some of the biggest names in Silicon Valley. And fashion designers are finding work in New York's fashion district making clothes for the biggest retailers in the world.

Other artistic careers offer different kinds of rewards. Landscape designers work outdoors and beautify public spaces while helping to improve the environment. Music therapists say that relieving their client's physical and mental pain with music provides a profound sense of joy that can't be found at a "regular" job.

Finding Your Inner Artist

The renowned painter and sculptor Pablo Picasso once said, "Every child is an artist. The problem is how to remain an artist once he grows up." When Picasso made that statement in the early 1970s, the modern digital world of personal computers, smartphones, software apps, and the World Wide Web did not yet exist. Today artistic kids have countless opportunities to exercise their talents and then use them in the work world when they grow up.

It might be true that software designers, microbiologists, and mathematicians have an easier time finding employment. But for artists, designers, and musicians the road to career happiness and prosperity is only limited by the imagination. And to quote Picasso once again, "Everything you imagine is real." So if you prefer thinking outside the box to working all day in a cubicle, a career in the arts might be your ticket to the future. If you imagine it, it might become a reality.

Graphic Designer

What Does a Graphic Designer Do?

If you surf the web, read a magazine, scan a menu at a restaurant, or check out a billboard ad along the highway, you're looking at the work of graphic designers. Graphic designers—or graphic artists—combine artistic talent with communication skills to convey messages in print and electronic media. Their creative skills include an eye for art and color, an understanding of type fonts, and knowledge of the way logos, photos, and other graphic elements come together in distinctive product designs. Graphic artists create advertisements, book covers, websites, layouts for newspapers and magazines, corporate reports, promotional displays, packaging, signage, and more. Some graphic designers work in much larger formats; they design billboards and graphic displays for vans, semitrailers, and even aircraft.

While the concept of combining text and images on a page or screen may seem simple, some graphic designers devise extremely creative ways to draw attention to their clients' messages. In 1999 when Austrian graphic designer Stefan Sagmeister was asked to create a poster for an event by the professional design organization AIGA he had one of his assistants carve the text into his skin using an X-Acto knife. He photographed the end result which was both shocking and attention grabbing. While most designers do not bleed for their clients, the work can be stressful as graphic arts director Craig Weiland explains on the Quora website: "At times, the job can be downright nerve-racking, and not everyone understands the amount of time that some projects take to produce. When raw copy and information is delivered to me late, incomplete or incorrect (or all of the above), it impinges on my sleep, my leisure time and my sanity." However, Weiland explains that when a project is successfully completed in spite of the setbacks, his clients view him as a "rock star" for his efforts.

How to Become a Graphic Designer

In his book best-selling *Outliers* author Malcolm Gladwell says it takes about ten thousand hours of practice to become a master in a given field—even if someone is not "naturally gifted." If your brain shuts down when you ponder the concept of practicing graphic design for ten thousand hours (that's eight hours a day for more than three years) consider another point made by Gladwell: Experts in any given field don't just work hard, they fall in love with their skill to the point that they want to do it all the time. So if you love to draw, paint, and take photos, if you love type fonts a little more than most, if you're fascinated with graphics and design software, putting the "art" in graphic artist won't feel like work.

So how do you hone your design skills? Writing for the Udemy website, designer Kimberly Pendergrass provides an answer: "Design is a skill, and like all skills, it can be learned." And design skills are acquired through practice. Pendergrass recommends keeping a notebook handy and using it to scribble pictures, cartoons, and fonts. Since graphic designers work with computers, sharpen your knowledge of industry-standard graphic design

Graphic designers combine artistic talent with communication skills to convey messages in print and electronic media. Their work requires a strong sense of color, knowledge of type fonts, and an understanding of how to combine various graphic elements to create distinctive product designs.

applications; you definitely need to understand Adobe Photoshop, Illustrator, and InDesign.

If you want to compete with the best, plan to learn the full Adobe Creative Suite which also includes Acrobat, Dreamweaver, Premiere, and After Effects. To really understand the intricacies of these programs, it might be helpful to visit your local library. Books like *Adobe Creative Suite 6 Design & Web Premium Classroom in a Book* can help you figure out the complexities of the software. And if you're on a limited budget and can't afford Adobe, there are free downloadable programs available online including GIMP, Scribus, Inkscape, and Pixlr.

Put your skills to work by making up an imaginary company, product, or musical group. "Brand" your product with logos, websites, T-shirt designs, and other graphic art. If you need inspiration study the work of graphic arts experts and pioneers. Do a web search of terms like "20 graphic designers you should know," "famous graphic artists," or "graphic art inspiration." And when you're starting out don't be afraid to take inspiration from the ideas of experts and add your own twist. While plagiarism (stealing ideas from others and calling them your own) can quickly ruin any career, almost all great artists take inspiration from those who came before them. As Pendergrass writes in her Udemy blog, "There are thousands of design books out there, full of amazing advice, sample work and tips from the best designers through the ages. . . . Learn from the best, then apply their principles, constantly, in your own work."

Do You Need a College Degree?

Most graphic design positions require a bachelor's degree in fine arts or design. According to the National Association of Schools of Art and Design there are about three hundred postsecondary institutions with programs in art and design. However, many schools require students to finish a year of basic art and design programs before they are allowed entry into a bachelor's degree program. These courses can be completed in high school. Most

"Everything I Ever Dreamed Of"

"I'm the art director for a $1.5 billion agricultural cooperative in the heartland of the U.S., and I'm doing everything I ever dreamed of and then some. In 2010, the cooperative rolled out its first major corporate rebranding in 30 years. I got to create the new logo and all its various permutations. . . . I designed livery for our fleet trucks and massive graphics for our 52' van trailers. I designed a new template for our print advertising, which is seen all over the Midwest. I designed our Web site, which gets visitors from all over the world."

Craig Weiland, "What's It Really like to Be a Graphic Designer?," *Mashable*, June 24, 2015. http://mashable.com.

art and design schools require students to submit sketches, designs, and other examples of their artistic ability.

Bachelor's degree programs in art and design include courses in principles of design, computerized design, communications design, commercial graphics production, studio art, printing techniques, and website design. In addition to design, courses in art history, writing, and foreign languages might prove useful in helping designers work effectively. If you are interested in launching a freelance career in graphic design, marketing and business courses are a must.

If your interests incline more toward the technical aspects of graphic design, consider attending a two-year community college or technical school to obtain an associate's degree in graphic design. Courses emphasize hands-on learning and tech skills focused on industry-related technology and software. Course topics include typography, illustration, interface design, and web development. An associate's degree allows a graduate to pursue entry-level jobs as a graphic designer or production artist.

Your Portfolio Is Your Job Ticket

By the time you finish school you should have a fairly large portfolio of design projects that you completed during your studies. You might also have examples of design work completed for family, friends, or freelance clients. You need to sort through this work and find the projects that present your creative abilities and technical skills in the most attractive light. The material needs to be perfected, polished, and presented on a dazzling website created specifically to highlight your graphic design skills.

Your website needs to be clean, uncluttered, and easy to use since most creative directors who hire at design agencies receive dozens of e-mails every day with links to portfolios and résumés. To deal with this tsunami of job seekers a creative director might spend thirty seconds clicking through the portfolio you so lovingly assembled. If your talents grab them, they might spend five or ten minutes checking out your work. "First impressions count and your website is the very first thing you're going to be judged on," award-winning design director and author Ram Castillo writes on the AIGA website. "How you present your work (i.e., the design and user experience of your website) is as important as the work itself, if not more."

The Work and Where It Can Lead

Most graphic designers work directly with clients whether they work at home or at a design firm. On a typical workday a client will hand a graphic designer a brief which describes a problem that needs to be solved or an outcome that the client hopes to achieve. The designer will brainstorm with the client, tossing out ideas while sketching rough prototypes of design concepts. Then the designer goes to work, analyzing the information and determining the best visual medium to deliver the client's message. Depending on the job, the designer will need to define the shapes, colors, fonts, photography, and animation for the project. The final execution might involve anything from setting up photo shoots to creating content for the piece to finalizing the design on a computer.

Design firms offer opportunities for advancement, and many graphic designers strive to become art directors. While the pay is better, the job of an art director is more demanding. Art directors work with many different people, including marketing directors, graphic artists, photographers, and executives. Depending on the company, they develop overall designs for products, packaging, print media, and web-based materials. Art directors must be extremely organized as they coordinate production artists, illustrators, and others to complete a project on time and to a client's satisfaction. That means art directors need to be available to everyone involved in a project. They must listen to employees' concerns and understand what they're trying to accomplish. Often a busy art director will come into the office on nights or weekends when it is quiet and they can concentrate on their own work.

Whether you're an entry-level graphic designer or an art director, the job requires more than skills; it requires humility. You might see your designs in magazines or on trucks flying down the highway, but do not expect public credit for your work. As Weiland explains on Quora: "When you put something out there for the world to see, you don't want the recognition. You want your client (or employer) to get it, and if they do, you've done your job right."

Freelancing and Finding a Niche

About 46 percent of graphic designers are freelancers, which means they work for themselves. To be a successful freelance graphic designer in this highly competitive field you need to be part designer and part salesperson. And keeping old clients and finding new ones can be a full-time task. As freelance web designer Grant Friedman explains on the ArtBistro website, "Designers who spend too much time chasing after leads can quickly find themselves with no time to actually design. Conversely, graphic designers who spend too much time designing may also find that they don't have enough clients to support the business."

To overcome this conflict Friedman recommends becoming a niche designer—someone who focuses on a specific product. A niche designer might only design T-shirts, package labels, logos, or banner ads. Or a niche might include an entire industry. There are, for example, designers who only work in the billboard industry or in real estate. By carving out a niche, a designer cuts down on the competition, which means better odds at landing a contract. Niche designers who are successful can find themselves in the enviable position of being considered an expert in a specific field. This means clients will come to you for advice and provide referrals to others in their particular business.

The Lowdown on a Career in Graphic Design

According to the Bureau of Labor Statistics there were more than 261,600 people working in the graphic design field in 2014. The field was expected to grow by only 1 percent a year through 2024, which means roughly 2,600 jobs will be added every year. Entry-level graphic designers can expect to earn around $23,000 a year, but those with a few years of experience earn an average of $45,900 a year. As you gain experience you might be promoted to a position like web graphics designer ($34,000 to $63,000), senior graphic designer (up to $78,000 a year), or art director (up to $86,000). While the statistics might not appear promising, a career in graphic design can provide an artistic outlet to those who prefer to work with color, design, and imagery.

Find Out More

AIGA
233 Broadway, 17th Floor
New York, NY 10279
phone: (212) 807-1990
website: www.aiga.org

The AIGA is the oldest and largest professional design organization. It works to advance design as a professional craft. The site hosts a career guide and links to design jobs for interns and professionals.

Color Marketing Group (CMG)

1908 Mount Vernon Ave.
Alexandria, VA 22301
phone: (703) 329-8500
website: www.colormarketing.org

The CMG is made up of color design professionals who apply their expertise to marketing and manufacturing. Its members interpret, create, forecast, and select colors in order to enhance the function, salability, and quality of manufactured goods. CMG members share their color expertise to provide information about color and design across all industries.

Society for Experiential Graphic Design (SEGD)

11900 L St. NW, Suite 710
Washington, DC 20036
phone: (202) 638-5555
website: https://segd.org

The SEGD is a global community of professionals from many artistic fields, including graphic and information designers, fabricators, architects, and exhibition designers. The website provides links to education programs and the SEGD student group which allows prospective designers to posts their résumés and sign up for mentor programs.

University & College Designers Association (UCDA)

199 Enon Springs Rd. W, Suite 400
Smyrna, TN 37167
phone: (615) 459-4559
website: https://ucda.com

The UCDA offers professional development opportunities to beginning designers through conferences, summits, and workshops; a quarterly trade publication; a monthly job-posting service; and more.

Multimedia Artist and Animator

What Does a Multimedia Artist and Animator Do?

The Bureau of Labor Statistics (BLS) combines multimedia artists and animators into one career group. People in the field create two- and three-dimensional models, animation, and visual effects for various forms of media. Multimedia artists use pens, ink, paint, computers, software, and other tools to give static images the illusion of motion.

To put art in motion multimedia artists draw on a combination of talents including artistic skill, creative inspiration, technological ability, and independent thinking. Multimedia artists are skilled in life and figure drawing and typically have a deep understanding of human and animal anatomy. They hone their drawing skills by watching live-action films of acrobats, dancers, wrestlers, reptiles, and even barnyard animals in order to accurately draw bodies in motion. Multimedia artists enhance their work by manipulating color, texture, light, and shadow in each series of drawings.

Multimedia artists are employed in a variety of fields. Some focus on creating animation for websites. Others work on animated movies, commercials, music videos, or video games. Multimedia artists who work with computer-generated images (CGI) create characters, environments, and special effects in 2D and 3D for movies and television shows.

Multimedia artists can further specialize. Some focus on creating only animated characters, while others concentrate on scenery or background design. One multimedia specialty involves animating from motion capture data, or mocap. This process involves digitally recording the movements of human actors and mapping them out on 3D software. Animators use this digital information to create computer-generated characters, like Gollum in *The Lord of the Rings: The Two Towers*.

How to Become a Multimedia Artist

If you love the arts and want to become a multimedia designer and animator you should take art classes and sharpen your drawing skills in color, perspective, and form. It is also important to learn the latest multimedia software programs like Autodesk 3ds Max, Adobe Creative Suite Master Collection, and LightWave 3D. Most importantly, try to develop your own artistic style. Scan the web to learn from the best and fill up your notebooks with sketches, character studies, and cartoons.

For a great real-life example of what it takes to become a successful multimedia artist, look no further than San Diego native Brian Schwab. He's a cutting-edge designer who owns a thriving multimedia design firm. Schwab took up drawing and sketching at a young age. By the time he was a teenager he was a skilled artist. While attending high school in 1997 Schwab took an extra-curricular multimedia art course where he learned to use Adobe software programs like Illustrator, Photoshop, and Premiere. After graduation, Schwab attended San Jose State University, where he obtained a bachelor of fine arts in digital media. Schwab taught for six years before opening his own firm, MyMediaDesigner, in 2008. On the Art Career Project website, Schwab extols the merits of his career: "I do what I love every day . . . every job is different and no two projects are the same."

A Love of Art and a College Degree

Some multimedia artists and animators find work on the strength of their portfolios alone. But most employers of multimedia artists and animators require their prospective hires to have a bachelor's degree in fine arts, animation, or computer graphics. To find work at a video game company, a degree in video game design or interactive media will help land a job.

Your Portfolio Is Your Job Ticket

Employers who hire multimedia artists and animators are looking for people with artistic ability, creativity, and technical proficiency. These talents are best displayed through a personal portfolio. Your portfolio should consist of a DVD or website that showcases your drawing and painting talents as well as your mastery of multimedia software.

Keep a Sketchbook

"I encourage all my students to get a sketchbook and draw as often as they can, no matter what their skill level is. This is very crucial for several reasons. First, it helps you start a regimen of observing people and capturing something about them that interests you. It really helps me as an animator when I can pull from direct observation and put it into a scene that I'm animating. Another reason why I feel that drawing is so crucial to good animation is that it has strengthened my eye for good poses, appeal, and clarity."

Bonnie Baglioli Randall, "Pixar's Chris Chua Discusses a Day in the Life of an Animator and How He Got There," Animations Career Review, December 19, 2011. www.animation careerreview.com.

Students enrolled in degree programs usually have portfolios that they created as part of their graduation requirements. But most employers see hundreds of class assignments and design projects every month. That's why experts recommend enhancing your portfolio with your own, unique short animation. A humorous or poignant story, artistically drawn and well told, will make a lasting impression and separate your work from the competition.

If you're applying for a job in computer animation, employers will want to see examples of drawings taken from life and direct observation. These include hands, feet, human figures, animals, and interior and exterior environments. But avoid clichés like dragons and unicorns. And don't overwhelm prospective employers with a portfolio featuring too much imagery or technical gimmicks. Tailor your portfolio to the position you're applying for with five to ten pieces that best demonstrate your style and skills.

While portfolios are important, many employers are also looking for what are called "soft skills." These skills, which are helpful in any job, include the ability to verbally communicate and to write clearly and effectively. People with soft skills pay full attention to what people are saying, take time to understand points being made, and ask appropriate questions.

A Day in the Life of a Multimedia Artist

Multimedia artists usually work in teams. Depending on the job, they work with directors, engineers, game designers, clients, and other artists. When projects are being developed, multimedia artists and animators brainstorm to come up with concepts and ideas. They use their drawing abilities to produce quick sketches to illustrate a project's general design. The multimedia artist then turns the sketches into detailed storyboards—large hand-drawn illustrations used during the initial stages of production to map out key scenes in an animated project.

Multimedia artists are often called upon to conduct extensive research into the visual elements of their specific project. For example, if an animation takes place in a jungle, the multimedia artist might study the plants, animals, and people living in the Amazon rain forest to create accurate portrayals.

When a project is in progress, multimedia artists will watch dailies. These short segments, produced every day, show a shot or series of shots. The dailies are viewed by all of the animators and producers on a team who then share their thoughts and criticism. After this session, the multimedia artist might go back and correct problems found in the dailies, or continue working on a project until the end of the day.

For those who work at major entertainment companies the work week often involves attending classes. Pixar, for instance, encourages its employees to attend Pixar University. This onsite education center includes technical training, art and film education, special guest lectures, and even health and recreation classes.

Best Career Cities for Multimedia Artists and Animators

There's plenty of competition among multimedia artists and animators hoping to be the next Seth MacFarlane (*Family Guy*) or Trey Parker (*South Park*). And while jobs in the field can be found in many cities, several places in North America have emerged as hubs for aspiring multimedia artists and animators.

California is home to more animators and multimedia artists than any other state in the nation. As the entertainment capital of the world, Los Angeles is at the top of the list for multimedia professionals. A complete list of L.A. studios would take up an entire book, but some of the most notable multimedia and animation producers include the Walt Disney Company, Acme Filmworks (producers of commercials and title sequences), Renegade Animation (Flash/Toon Boom animation), Cartoon Network, FOX TV Animation, and many more. As journalist Robin Wilding explains on the Animation Careers Review website: "The City of Angels is a true mecca for animators. . . . Those lucky enough to score positions with the large animation firms in the area get to work with the top animators and producers in the industry."

Letting Design Juices Flow

"I wake up early and charge into my office; converse with my to-do list, update the whiteboard, and list out my challenges for the day. I like to write down more tasks that I can complete to keep me going, but if I didn't have my to-do list I would be lost, it's crucial. I try to take breaks, perform yoga, listen to Pandora and let the design juices flow. I am probably on the phone twice a week with Hosting Support, but I have learned a lot this way."

Brian Schwab, "Multimedia Designer," Art Career Project, 2016. www.theartcareerproject .com.

The San Francisco Bay Area is home to several world-famous entertainment companies as well as tech companies and video game makers who employ multimedia artists. Industrial Light & Magic, founded by filmmaker George Lucas, is located in the Presidio on the northern tip of the city. Across the Bay in Emeryville you have Pixar Animation Studios, producers of high-grossing animated features like *Monsters University* and the *Toy Story* films.

One of the Bay Area's largest employers is video game producer EA Games, located in Redwood City which is also home to the film studio DreamWorks. And the major studios aren't the only game in town. In recent years numerous boutique studios have opened, offering employment opportunities to multimedia and animation artists. There are also numerous world-class advertising and public relations agencies in San Francisco, like Ogilvy & Mather, which hire multimedia artists. While the cost of living is high in the Bay Area, local companies pay a premium for top talent, with salaries running from $90,000 to $110,000—the highest average in the country.

New York City is home to the second-largest film and video industry in the United States and several thousand people work in the entertainment industry as multimedia artists and animators. New York also employs around twenty-five hundred people who work in game design. The city is home to dozens of major players like Viacom and Nickelodeon, as well as hundreds of boutique and indie studios. And New York is the epicenter of the advertising and public relations industries. While thousands of multimedia artists come to New York City every year hoping to catch a break, the city also produces plenty of homegrown talent; New York has a number of highly ranked schools including Parsons at the New School for Design, the Tisch School of the Arts at NYU, and the School of Visual Arts (SVA).

The Lowdown on a Career as a Multimedia Artist

According to the BLS employment of multimedia artists and animators is projected to grow 6 percent through 2024, slightly slower than the average for all occupations. Projected growth will be due to increased demand for animation and visual effects in video games, movies, and television. The industries that employed the most multimedia artists and animators in 2014 were the motion picture and video industries; computer systems design and related services; software publishers; and advertising, public relations, and related services.

The median pay nationwide for multimedia artists and animators was $61,370. But salaries were higher in various states. The average in California was $82,170 per year. Multimedia artists and animators in New York could expect to earn $70,660, while those working in the state of Washington brought in an average of $75,740. The top 10 percent of multimedia artists earned more than $113,470.

Find Out More

Academy of Interactive Arts & Sciences (AIAS)
11175 Santa Monica Blvd., 4th Floor
Los Angeles, CA 90025
phone: (310) 484-2560
website: www.interactive.org

The AIAS has several scholarship programs established to support students who are pursuing careers in interactive entertainment.

AIGA Nashville

AIGA Nashville
PO Box 150201
Nashville, TN 37215
e-mail: president@nashville.aiga.org
website: http://nashville.aiga.org

AIGA Nashville is an organization of designers, design educators, creative directors, photographers, illustrators, web designers, multimedia artists, animators, and other creative professionals. The website features links to job openings and provides information on job market trends.

Art Career Project

2926 Juniper St.
San Diego, CA 92104
e-mail: editor@theartcareerproject.com
website: www.theartcareerproject.com

This site is hosted by artists working to help others find careers in graphic design, painting, photography, video game design, and other artistic fields.

ASIFA-Hollywood

2114 W. Burbank Blvd.
Burbank, CA 91506
e-mail: info@asifa-hollywood.org
website: www.asifa-hollywood.org

The Hollywood chapter of the International Animated Film Society promotes and encourages the art and craft of animation by supporting animation education. ASIFA-Hollywood hosts the annual Annie Awards to honor individuals who have made significant contributions to the art of animation. The organization also has an extensive animation archive at its Burbank facility.

Graphic Artists Guild, Inc.
31 W. Thirty-Fourth St., 8th Floor
New York, NY 10001
phone: (212) 791-3400
website: https://graphicartistsguild.org

The Graphic Artists Guild serves graphic and interactive designers, illustrators, animators, web programmers, and developers of all skill levels. The website offers guidelines for assembling portfolios, notices of art competitions, and other topics of interest to graphic arts students.

Fashion Designer

What Does a Fashion Designer Do?

Anyone who wants to understand the life of a fashion designer only needs to tune in to the hit TV show *Project Runway*. Although it is a reality show, *Project Runway* encapsulates the life of a fashion designer in the real world. Most of the contestants on the show are freelance fashion designers. To get a chance to compete designers must wow the judges with impressive pieces from their fashion collections. Once they are accepted to appear on the show, the contestants labor under very stressful conditions. Long hours are spent sketching patterns, cutting cloth, sewing, and dyeing. And the opinions of the judges when the garments are seen on the runway can be unforgiving—much like clothing buyers and fashion magazine editors in the real world. Plenty of tears are shed, but for those who succeed, the rewards are many. The work of winners on *Project Runway* can appear on the pages of *Marie Claire* and on racks in the nation's largest department stores.

As *Project Runway* host Heidi Klum often says on the show, "In

Seeing a Piece Come Together

"There's a knock at the door—it's a young model who's come for a fitting. I try her in some of the most up-to-date toiles [test garments], adjusting hemlines and sleeve lengths where necessary–and trying not to prick her with the pins. Just before the model has to leave, I dress her in one of the season's completed designs. When you spend so long thinking about a collection, even though you've seen endless samples and patterns, there is nothing more satisfying and uplifting than seeing a finished piece come together."

Charlotte Simpson, "A Day in the Life of Fashion Designer Charlotte Simpson," *Harper's Bazaar*, September 4, 2013. www.harpersbazaar.co.uk.

fashion, one day you're in. And the next day, you're out." Despite the fickle nature of the business thousands of people dream of becoming the next Michael Kors or Donna Karan. And fashion designers play a central role in the clothing business.

Americans buy over 20 billion garments a year, close to seventy pieces of clothing per person. Although 98 percent of those garments are made in other countries, most designers have their offices in the United States. And while almost everyone has heard of Coco Chanel and Ralph Lauren, most of those billions of garments were designed by people whose names are largely unknown. They work for large apparel producers and design women's, men's, and children's clothing, including sportswear, maternity wear, outerwear, underwear, formal wear, eyewear, and footwear. Some fashion designers specialize in accessories such as hosiery, handbags, scarves, and belts.

Whether a fashion designer works for a large company like Old Navy or is a freelancer with private clients, the work is similar. Fashion designers sketch clothing designs, make patterns and sew, and study fashion trends; and are well acquainted with different types of fabrics and garment production.

Most fashion designers oversee every aspect of a design from the initial sketch to the manufacturing. They visit fabric producers to select cloth and trims, conduct fittings on prototype garments, and coordinate production of the final product.

The process of producing a garment from initial concept to clothing store takes up to eighteen months—and styles change at a rapid pace. This requires a fashion designer to be somewhat psychic; they need to predict what will be fashionable in the future. Some conduct their own research, while others rely on predictions published by trade industry groups. These trend reports describe what colors, fabrics, and styles will likely be popular in the coming seasons.

How to Become a Fashion Designer

Those who succeed in fashion design are people who were obsessed with clothing and styles at an early age. Kors is one such example; he redesigned his mother's wedding dress for her second marriage at the age of six. By the time he was ten, Kors says, "I practically hyperventilated every month when Vogue [magazine] arrived, and I loved shopping." Kors attended the Fashion Institute of Technology in New York City, but only for two semesters. However, after he dropped out he continued to study fashion trends, sketch clothing designs, and learn about fabrics and garment production while running his own New York City boutique.

Fashion design is an incredibly competitive field. Carol Mongo, of Parsons School of Design in Paris, recommends that prospective fashion designers get a lot of sewing experience in high school. They should also perfect their drawing skills, since drawings are the way designers communicate their ideas. Art classes can help an aspiring fashionista understand body form and proportion. But the most important thing a fashion designer needs cannot be learned in schools, as Mongo writes on the Fashion Net website: "We can't teach you how to be creative—you have to bring your creativity to us and let us lead you on your way."

Do You Need a College Degree?

While many successful designers have little or no college education, most entry-level jobs require a bachelor's of fine arts degree in fashion. In the same article Mongo points out: "We live in a brandname society, and having the name of a good school [on your résumé] really does help." At schools like Parsons, successful designers work directly with graduating students. In addition, students learn more than the creative side of design—they also take business classes to learn about clothing business economics, contracts, picking business partners, and running ad campaigns.

A degree can help you perfect your sewing and pattern-making skills and teach you about fashion history and trends, textiles, patterns, and colors. On the StyleCaster website, designer and blogger Christina explains the importance of higher education: "With an academic background in fashion design, students can better understand the garment production process, improve functionality, fit and aesthetics in their designs for specific clients, and meet and anticipate consumer demands."

Your Portfolio Is Your Job Ticket

To get into a good fashion school or find a job in fashion design, you need to assemble a good portfolio. Your portfolio should demonstrate the scope of your output, your skills and experience, and how you generate and execute your designs. A fashion designer's portfolio should contain technical drawings called fashion flats—finished designs on fashion presentation boards—and three to six collections presented on six fashion figures, sketches of models with elongated proportions that are the standard forms used in the industry. Each collection should start off with an inspiration page consisting of a collage of images and fabric swatches to demonstrate the mood and color story of the collection. If you include photos of your collection, they should be of good quality. While hiring models and professional photographers is expensive, you might be able to barter or trade garments in exchange for their services.

Portfolios are meant to show off your best work, but one of the most common mistakes is filling it with all of your wildest fashion illustrations, photographs, and garments. The problem is that if you're applying for an entry-level position at a large company, no one needs to see your avant-garde fashion designs because no one buys those styles in the real world. Instead tailor your portfolio to the company where you're applying. What is the company's design philosophy? Who buys their clothes? What does their current collection look like? Once you understand that, ask yourself what the company might be looking for in a fashion designer. Your portfolio should show prospective employers that you have an eye for their style and that you can create a cohesive collection that they would be happy to produce.

Once you have assembled your portfolio, you need to draw on your writing skills. Your collections should have stories: where you found your inspiration and why your clothing is unique or fashion forward. On the Creative Bloq website Luke O'Neill, art director of *T3* magazine, explains the importance of a good portfolio story: "There's nothing worse than going through someone's portfolio who has little or nothing to say about their work. Ensure that all the pieces that you include are ones that you're very proud of and can talk confidently and enthusiastically about in a meeting, explaining the back story and journey you went through to get there."

A Day in the Life of a Fashion Designer

Most fashion designers create clothing for wholesalers or manufacturers who sell garments throughout the world. While their designs might be worn by millions of people, their names are unknown. But they work in comfortable settings at regular hours.

A small number of designers work in the high-fashion, or haute couture, industry. Most are self-employed. These designers might create high-priced custom clothing for individual clients. Other haute couture designers sell their designs in their own boutiques or to specialty shops and expensive department stores. Freelance fashion design can be stressful; designers have to cultivate clients (and keep them happy), pay for their own studios and equipment, and juggle artistic and business duties. And most freelance fashion designers only get paid every six months, once each season when products are delivered to stores.

Wherever a fashion designer works, the process of creating clothes from scratch is similar. Most garments come to life on a sketchpad. The sketch provides a blueprint for the designer to cut pieces of cloth and assemble them into a garment on a mannequin, or "dummy." Designers are increasingly using computer-aided design (CAD) software which allows them to look at their work on virtual models and change the colors, fabric patterns, and shapes of the garment before putting it into production.

Once the sketches are finalized the designer creates a rough working pattern. This is often done by cutting pieces of an inexpensive material like muslin. The cloth is then pinned together on a mannequin. This allows the designer to see how the garment drapes, or hangs.

Designers who work at large fashion houses will hand their prototype garment to skilled pattern makers, tailors, and sewers who create master patterns used by clothing manufacturers.

Designers who freelance or work at smaller fashion houses often do the pattern making and sewing themselves.

The highlight of a fashion designer's job is the fashion show. Designers are in control of every step when they exhibit their collection on a runway; they select the clothing, models, accessories, music, runway backdrops, and the order in which the garments are shown. The epitome of success for a fashion designer is to show a collection at New York Fashion Week, held in February and September each year. During Fashion Week international collections are shown to buyers, celebrities, the press, and the general public. Fashion Weeks are also held in Paris, Milan, and London at different times of the year.

The Lowdown on a Career as a Fashion Designer

Competition for jobs in fashion design is strong and the garment industry is not for the faint of heart. But for those who can compete, the rewards are great. According to *Business Insider* if you have an art degree and "want to go where the money is, you'll set your sights on becoming a fashion designer." *Business Insider* says the job of chief fashion designer topped the list of highest-paying jobs for art majors in 2015, with an average median pay of $120,000. Senior fashion designers, who work under chief fashion designers, were paid $98,000. A fashion designer just starting a career could expect to earn $36,700.

Find Out More

Business of Fashion (BOF)
23-31 Great Titchfield St., 6th Floor
London W1W 7PA United Kingdom
website: www.businessoffashion.com

The BOF is considered essential daily reading for fashion designers. The website delivers news from fashion writers and insiders from style capitals around the world. The Careers link provides tips, informative articles, and job listings.

StyleCareers

4579 Laclede Ave., Suite 172
St Louis, MO 63108
phone: (314) 454-9920
website: www.stylecareers.com

StyleCareers is the largest fashion-only job listing site on the Internet, with offers in apparel, beauty, accessories, textiles, home fashion and more. The site provides a detailed view of real-world conditions in the style industry.

Vogue

1 World Trade Center
New York, NY 10007
phone: (212) 286-2860
website: www.vogue.com

Vogue has been the world's most influential fashion magazine almost since its founding in 1892. The magazine's website is overflowing with valuable information for any up-and-coming designer, featuring articles on fashion, beauty, lifestyle, culture, and more.

Women's Wear Daily

475 Fifth Ave., 3rd Floor
New York, NY 10017
phone: (212) 213-1900
website: http://wwd.com

Women's Wear Daily is often called "the fashion bible," and its popular website is filled with information every aspiring fashion designer needs to know, including coveted fashion jobs on its career site.

Photographer

A Few Facts

Number of Jobs

In 2014 there were approximately 124,900 jobs in the field of photography.

Salaries

The median pay for a photographer in 2015 was $31,710 per year.

Educational Requirements

Photojournalists need a bachelor of arts degree; science and medical photographers need a bachelor of science degree in their chosen field.

Work Settings

Indoors and outdoors

Future Job Outlook

According to the Bureau of Labor Statistics, 3 percent growth a year through 2024

What Does a Photographer Do?

The word photography is derived from two Greek words: *photos* or "light," and *graphos* or "writing." Photography literally means "light writing" or "writing with light." This prompted George Eastman, who founded the photography company Kodak, to give this eloquent advice to photographers: "Light makes photography. Embrace light. Admire it. Love it. But above all, know light. Know it for all you are worth, and you will know the key to photography."

Eastman made his statement in the 1920s but his words are still important to those who work as professional photographers in the digital age. A professional photographer's job involves using the tools of the trade to take artistic pictures of people, places, and things. They use their creativity to compose images that tell a story or document an event. The best photographs elicit emotions in viewers, evoking feelings of happiness, disappointment, anxiety, wonderment, longing, or exhilaration.

The photographer's job also has many technical aspects. Photographers need to understand the complex functions of various types of digital cameras, lenses, lens filters, artificial lighting, memory cards, and exposure meters. Photographers also need a good working knowledge of image editing software like Photoshop, Pixelmator, or GIMP in order to manipulate light, shadow, color, and other elements in photographs to improve their appearance. As fine art photographer Michael Kenna puts it, "I think photography can be a curious mix of both logical thinking and wild imagination."

About 63 percent of photographers are self-employed; they need basic business skills as well as artistic and technical capacities. Self-employed photographers must advertise, sell their services to clients, set prices, keep business records, and maintain office and studio spaces.

Finding a Specialty

If you want to delve into the field of photography it is important to have a clear focus on the specific type of photographs you wish to sell. In an interview on the We Are Art People website, photojournalist Nick Stern says, "You should know EXACTLY . . . who you want to have as clients. Plan it out, write a goal or business plan then analyze how you can get there. Get mentored by people already there."

Prospective photographers can chose to specialize in many different fields. Stern is a photojournalist; he shoots pictures of newsworthy events like natural disasters and civil unrest. Nature photographers work outdoors shooting landscapes, wildlife, or even underwater; they travel, hike, climb, camp, and dive to capture unique shots of animals and scenery. Fashion or "glamour" photographers take photos of professional and amateur models and their clothes and accessories. They need to be experts in lighting their subjects to create the most flattering photos and often direct models to assume different poses. Other photographic fields include taking pictures of buildings for real estate sales and photographing medical subjects for research purposes. Forensic photographers record evidence at crime scenes. Event photographers specialize in shooting weddings, graduations, and similar occasions.

Microscopic photographers are those with an eye for the smallest details. They attach their cameras to microscopes to take photos called micrographs of algae, bacteria, crystals, fungi, insects, viruses, and other tiny objects. The photos are used by scientists in research work but can also have artistic value.

Do You Need a College Degree?

Photographers rely on creativity, a "good eye," and an understanding of the photographic process. And since most photographers are self-employed a college degree is not necessarily required. Many successful photographers recommend hands-on involvement, as Stern explains on We Are Art People: "Get out and take photos, nothing is better than learning from experience. Learn from your photos that 'don't work', look at them and consider why they don't work. Also look at great photos and think why they work so well."

Part of the photographic learning process might involve taking classes that cover technical aspects of photography, equipment, marketing, and software. Basic art courses include principles of photography, image manipulation, and location photography. Business, marketing, and accounting classes are helpful for self-employed photographers.

Those who wish to earn more money, working as photojournalists for example, should obtain a bachelor of arts degree. Scientific and medical photographers require a bachelor of science degree. Forensic photographers do not require a degree but are required in many states to complete law-enforcement courses in photography, processing, and forensics.

Your Portfolio Is Your Job Ticket

Whether your goal is to get into an art school to study photography or find jobs working for magazine editors or other clients, you will be judged by the quality of the photographs in your portfolio. A portfolio consists of a photographer's strongest work, but it also should have a unifying theme or style tailored to each client. For example, if a photographer is trying to get work displayed in an art gallery, the portfolio might consist of arty, attention-grabbing photos that shock or please the viewer. Someone hoping to get wedding work would have their portfolio anchored by event-related photos. Photographers seeking work in a number of different fields will assemble several portfolios. Each portfolio will be aimed at a specific audience whether it is editors of wildlife magazines or art directors at ad agencies.

The best way to assemble a portfolio is to start with about one hundred shots and winnow it down to the best twenty to thirty. Since most photographers are not the best judges of their own work it is best to get help from an impartial person whose judgment you trust. The final photos should be tastefully displayed on a website. Links should provide other info, including a list of all the photos in the portfolio, thumbnail contact sheets, and titles, dates, and locations for each shot. While some photographers prefer to let their work do all the talking, others include an artistic statement that outlines the thought processes behind the pictures. However, keep background information brief; you want people looking at the photos—not reading details about your forest photo shoot in the rain.

A Day in the Life of a Photographer

Photographers rarely have typical workdays; how they spend their time depends on the specific assignment. Jim Stephenson is a London freelancer who documents architecture, interiors, and the built environment. As Stephenson told *Darwin Magazine*, his work life "varies massively from day to day." When Stephenson is on a photo shoot, he will travel to a site and get to know the place by walking around the grounds and viewing the subject from as many angles as possible. Once he starts taking pictures he thinks of nothing else. At times he has even instructed his assistant to remind him to stop and eat lunch.

Stephenson works out of a home office so when a job is finished his time is spent editing photographs, e-mailing clients, and taking care of other photography business. After working all day, he might continue work on some of his easier tasks, like updating his Facebook page. While Stephenson works longer hours than he would at a regular job, he believes the freedom of freelancing is worth it: "I went freelance because I was attracted by the idea of doing my own thing and making the decisions. . . . I work longer hours now and probably take less holiday, but everything I do during my day is for me and my work."

Photographers like Stephenson work in urban areas, while other photographers spend their workdays in altogether different settings. Joel Sartore is a Nebraska-based freelance wildlife photographer. He travels the world to take stunning wildlife photos for *National Geographic*. His work can be dangerous; he's been chased by a 700-pound (318 kg) grizzly bear and dodged the massive horns of an enraged musk ox. When he's working, he gets up very early to get into position for shooting animals that begin feeding at sunrise. He might sit in one place until nightfall

It's Not About the Money

"It's important to be curious about life, to be pleasant and to try and make sure you're in photography for the right reasons. If you're in it for money and recognition, you're going to be sorely disappointed especially when starting out. Some people shoot great pictures for years and are only "discovered" after they die. If you're in it to make the world a better place by photographing and documenting important subjects, making people happy with your images, and making others see the world in a different way, chances are you'll enjoy a long and healthy career."

Mark Goldstein, "An Interview with Wildlife Photographer Joel Sartore," *Photography* (blog), March 23, 2010. www.photographyblog.com.

waiting for the perfect shot. He puts up with the discomfort because he is a man on a mission. As Sartore stated in an interview with Photography Blog: "I've always been really interested in endangered species. It's a matter of life and death, quite literally, and so the race is on to save them. My job is to get the public to first become aware that these creatures exist, then get them to care."

Working with Social Media

Most photographers use social media to promote their work. They have professional Facebook pages that anyone can access without being "friended." Photographers use these pages to display their latest work, announce special events like gallery showings, post blogs, offer tips and advice to customers, and share behind-the-scenes info, like what goes on at an outdoor shoot. Some photographers pay to advertise on Facebook to target users outside their social networks.

While YouTube is the world's premier video-sharing website, it is also the second-largest search engine—the site processes 3 billion searches a month. Photographers are using YouTube to display slide shows of their work and videos that show people how to take better pictures or what to expect at a portrait shoot. For example, photographer Peter Hurley created a fifteen-minute video that explains how specific facial expressions help people look more confident in portraits. Hurley posted the video in 2013, and by 2016 it had been viewed more than 2.3 million times. Such videos help build the photographer's reach and reputation. The videos allow people to get to know and trust the photographer and can be used to direct viewers to the photographer's personal website where prospective customers can purchase photos or book studio sessions.

The Lowdown on a Career in Photography

Earning a living as a photographer is difficult in an era when nearly everyone has a cell phone camera in their pocket or purse. Facebook reports that over 300 million photos are uploaded to the site every day—136,000 per minute. That means that anyone who really wants to do this kind of work will need to hustle. But in 2014 around 124,900 people worked as professional photographers and the field was growing, if slowly.

The median pay for a photographer in 2015 was $31,710 per year. Despite the rather low wages photography is an attractive job to many people. It's an accessible career; it can be pursued with a relatively small investment in a good camera, lights, and lenses. Photography is also current; the Internet constantly demands cutting-edge content, and photographers can provide images to new magazines and websites being created every day. And freelance photographers are their own bosses who can dictate their own hours and exercise total control over their careers.

Find Out More

American Society of Media Photographers (ASMP)
150 N. Second St.
Philadelphia, PA 19106
phone: (215) 451-2767
website: www.asmp.org

The ASMP was founded to protect and promote the interests of professional photographers and provide business resources. Students and freelancers can benefit from the seminars and webinars offered to members.

Association of International Photography Art Dealers (AIPAD)
2025 M Street NW, Suite 800
Washington, DC 20036
phone: (202) 367-1158
website: www.aipad.com

The AIPAD encourages public support of fine art photography by acting as a voice for the dealers in fine art photography. The organization is also committed to providing education about fine art photography to those in the photographic community.

National Press Photographers Association (NPPA)
120 Hooper St.
Athens, GA 30602
phone: (706) 542-2506
website: www.nppa.org

The NPPA advocates for the working news photographer, videographer, and multimedia journalist in the Internet age. The organization hosts a photojournalism contest, offers numerous photo and video workshops, and provides a wide range of information to help photographers improve their job prospects.

Professional Photographers of America (PPA)
229 Peachtree St. NE, Suite 2200
Atlanta, GA 30303
phone: (800) 786-6277
website: www.ppa.com

The PPA is the world's largest nonprofit photography association with more than twenty-nine thousand members in fifty countries. The association is focused on helping photographers succeed and offers links to networking sites, "Find a Photographer" job listings, and PPA affiliate schools.

Society for Photographic Education (SPE)
2530 Superior Ave. #403
Cleveland, OH 44114
phone: (216) 622-2733

The SPE promotes an understanding of photography as a means of diverse creative expression, cultural insight, and experimental practice through teaching, learning, scholarship, and criticism.

Landscape Designer

What Does a Landscape Designer Do?

Most people who pick a career in landscape design do so because they have an artistic streak and they love plants and nature. Landscape designers, whose work involves planning and installing gardens, are definitely not in it for the glory. On any given day a landscape designer can be found hauling plants and bags of mulch at a garden store, toiling outdoors in inclement weather, or digging up weeds under a broad-brimmed hat while dodging bugs and poison ivy. But some landscape designers have become TV stars; Chris Lambton is the host of *Yard Crashers* on the HGTV network. Lambton haunts home improvement stores on weekends, searching for gardeners who need a pro's advice. When he finds willing guests, Lambton "crashes" their yard for a few days and gives backyard gardens an expert makeover.

Although Lambton is one of the lucky few landscapers who is also a TV personality, he has much in common with less prominent landscape designers, as he mentioned in an interview with the YP website: "I would say my

Don't Be Afraid to Ask Questions

"Shopping for plants at your local nursery can be overwhelming, but it doesn't have to be. I suggest you begin by introducing yourself to one of the knowledgeable staff members and that you continue to go to them with questions. Use their expertise in figuring out where to plant the items you want. Just ask questions, and you will learn in no time."

Gregg Rosenzweig, "Landscaping Tips from HGTV's Chris Lambton," YP, October 8, 2012. www.yellowpages.com.

landscape design philosophy is finding beauty in nature. . . . I think people have forgotten how beautiful nature is and are too often stuck inside. I want to get them back outside where they can experience nature and hang out with friends and family."

If you possess artistic skills and an eye for beauty, and wish to become an expert on plants, shrubs, trees, and flowers, landscape design might be your ticket to a career in the great outdoors. Landscape designers create plans for gardens, walkways, fountains, outdoor lighting, and other features. They oversee garden construction in residential yards, public parks, playgrounds, golf courses, college campuses, and shopping centers. Landscape designers work with homeowners, corporate clients, urban planners, park supervisors, and public agencies.

The landscape designer's artistic canvas is the natural world, anything outdoors—in both rural and urban areas—where people interact with the environment. When designing landscapes they draw from a broad range of talents and technical skills. Some landscape designers use colored pencils, watercolors, and acrylic paint to create detailed drawings, diagrams, and plans for gardens. Designers also work on computers using outdoor design software apps, including RealTime Landscaping and Home Designer Suite. Landscape designers must also be deft at promoting their work in local papers and on social media, and taking care of basic business and accounting tasks.

One of the biggest trends in landscape design is environmental sustainability—emphasizing the use of native plants and shunning pesticides, herbicides, and other agricultural chemicals. Sustainable landscape designers work to preserve the natural environment, improve air and water quality, and conserve power, among other objectives. To attain these goals they use recycled construction materials and promote the use of rainwater harvesting systems and solar panels. Sustainable designers believe that features like rooftop gardens, bike trails, and community vegetable gardens should be part of every urban landscape.

Advancing Your Career

In most states landscape designers are not required to hold special permits or work certificates to perform their jobs. However, landscape designers hoping to advance their careers can attend accredited landscape architecture schools to become landscape architects. Landscape architects are educated in urban planning, architecture, horticulture, geology, and civil and structural engineering. They work with surveyors, engineers, environmental researchers, and other architects. Professionals in the landscape architecture field generally work on large commercial or public projects like the Mississippi riverfront in Minneapolis, High Line Park in Manhattan, and Gas Works Park in Seattle.

How to Become a Landscape Designer

The paintings that French artist Claude Monet made in his garden in Giverny, France, are among the world's most famous artworks. Monet was a master painter, but he was also a talented landscape designer who spent long hours in the late-nineteenth century paging through seed catalogs and discussing plant specimens with French gardening experts. He planted a garden with a riotous array of foliage; the flowers, trees, and bushes were strategically placed to emphasize their textures, colors, and shapes. Today Monet's garden is a national monument visited by half a

A landscape designer chooses plants that will bring out the look and feel of her design. Developing pleasing designs for residential yards, public parks, shopping centers, and more requires an eye for beauty and knowledge of plants, lighting, fountains, and other landscape features.

million tourists every year. And the visual impact of the garden provides artistic inspiration to landscape designers everywhere.

While you don't need to be Claude Monet to pursue a career in landscape design, art classes are important. Many landscape designs begin with hand-drawn sketches that envision three-dimensional spaces, color-coordinated gardens, fountains, walkways, and other features. Beyond the creative arts, a prospective landscape designer or architect needs to focus on at least three of the four STEM topics—science, engineering, and math. The science aspect includes learning about botany, biology, geology, chemistry, and environmental sciences. Engineering and math are important for architectural planning, creating blueprints, and designing structures. And of course math is important for anyone hoping to run their own business, along with communication and computer skills.

Do You Need a College Degree?

In many states a person can become a landscape designer simply by printing up business cards and finding clients to pay them for the work. However, bachelor's degree programs in landscape design provide instruction in basic design principles such as planning and implementation, environmental stewardship, and professional practices. Many undergraduate programs require students to complete a project that demonstrates their proficiency in the design process from start to finish.

Your Portfolio Is Your Job Ticket

Most landscape designers find work by assembling a powerful, dynamic portfolio that features their drawings, plans, letters of recommendation, and photos of completed projects. But if you're just starting out as a landscape designer you might not have references or completed projects to feature in a portfolio. That shouldn't slow you down. There are hundreds of informative gardening websites with pictures and plans that can provide inspiration. Creativity is the name of the game; use your art materials and download some free landscape design software to create your own digital Giverny for your portfolio. You can also get digging by joining a garden club, volunteering to work with an established landscape designer, or doing some free gardening work for a relative or neighbor.

A portfolio is meant to showcase your strongest work and provide a testament to your design talents. You should use your portfolio to instill trust by explaining your background, passion for plants, awards, and whatever landscape design accomplishments you might have. The sketches and photographs in your portfolio should illustrate your vision and dreams. If you do volunteer work keep track of your expenditures and schedule so you can demonstrate that you have the skills to complete projects on time and within a budget.

When designing a portfolio, the introductory page should make a good first impression. It should feature eye-catching material that engages viewers and makes them want to know more about you as a designer. A few well-written biographical sentences should make the viewer wish to explore further. Computer animations can be used to show how a design will be constructed from start to finish or how a garden will grow to maturity. Once a portfolio is completed it needs to be posted online where clients can find it. Most landscape designers use social media like Facebook, Instagram, and Twitter to exhibit examples of their work and provide links to their portfolios.

A Day in the Life of a Landscape Designer

Most landscape designers are self-employed or work for small firms. A typical day in the life of a landscape designer is taken up by two main elements: design and implementation. Design tasks take place in a home office or office suite where the designer meets with new clients to learn what they want. Whenever a new project gets started the designer needs to ask questions. How much time does the client spend in the yard? What are the client's favorite colors and plants? How big is the space, and is it sunny or shady? How much money does the client want to invest in the project? Do they want a low-maintenance yard or a yard that requires a great deal of care? Washington, DC, landscape designer Tom Noll explains the need to ask many detailed questions: "You know, when you're landscaping somebody's house, you really want to get across to them that the landscaping is really a part of them. That's what people see before they see you. How do you want to come across to those people: do you just want simple landscaping that doesn't matter, or do you want to portray your personality?"

During the initial process, landscape designers visit the proposed site where they take detailed measurements of lot elevation, width, and length. With this information the designer might create up to three different designs for a client, each one at a different estimated price. The plans will either be hand-drawn sketches or complete conceptual designs created on a computer with landscape design software. The software allows designers to make future time projections which lets clients see what a space will look like in five to ten years. When plans are completed, the landscape designer will meet with the client to provide price quotes, discuss changes, and settle on project completion dates.

Before work begins, the designer will take soil samples from the site and send them for analysis by a soil biologist. This process determines the texture, density, nutrients, organic matter, and other aspects of the soil. With this knowledge the landscape designer can prepare the soil to ensure that the new plants will thrive. Landscape designers working onsite also make note of drainage, nearby water features like ponds and streams, and other characteristics that will impact the site.

Once the project moves forward the landscape designer will adjust cost estimates, create a project plan, and hire landscape contractors to complete the work. As the project takes shape the landscape designer acts as a project manager, visiting the site regularly and ensuring that the plans are being executed properly.

Understanding Design and Human Nature

"Landscape design is a lot like other 'design' fields, governed by principles such as form, contrast, hierarchy, rhythm, line, color and so on. . . . Landscape designers need comprehensive knowledge of a broad palette of materials, from plants to paving materials, finishes, textiles, lighting and furnishings. . . . Obviously, we need to understand our clients' wishes, and local environmental conditions. But the best landscape designers I know evoke rich emotional responses with very simple and subtle gestures. And to achieve that, we must understand human nature—what people respond to, what brings us pleasure."

Cindy Dyer, "Interview: John Black, Landscape Designer," *Cindy Dyer's Blog*, November 5, 2011. https://cindydyer.wordpress.com.

Some landscape designers dig in and get their hands dirty to help complete a project. Once the project is complete most landscape designers remain in touch with their clients. The designers might return to the project on an annual or semiannual basis to make sure plants are thriving and the landscape is maturing as planned.

The Lowdown on a Career as a Landscape Designer

According to the Bureau of Labor Statistics landscape designers earned an annual average salary of $42,315 in 2015. Landscape architects earned about $68,570. Due to new construction and a growing interest in gardens and native plants the field of landscape design is expected to grow by 14 percent through 2022. California employed the most landscape designers, while those working in Hawaii and the District of Columbia received the highest pay.

Find Out More

American Society of Landscape Architects (ASLA)
636 I St. NW
Washington, DC 20001
phone: (202) 898-2444
website: www.asla.org

The ASLA is the national professional association for landscape architects; it has members in forty-nine professional chapters and seventy-two student chapters. The "Learn" link on the website provides information about resources, conferences, and other educational opportunities.

Association of Professional Landscape Designers (APLD)
2207 Forest Hills Dr.
Harrisburg, PA 17112
phone: (717) 238-9780
website: www.apld.org

The APLD is dedicated to advancing the profession of landscape design. The APLD website provides links to helpful resources for prospective designers such as the American Garden Archives of the Smithsonian Institution.

International Federation of Landscape Architects (IFLA)
Avenue Louise 149/24, 12th Floor
B-1050 Brussels, Belgium
phone: 32.495.568.285
website: http://iflaonline.org

The mission of the IFLA is to create globally sustainable and balanced living environments for the benefit of humanity worldwide. The IFLA educational affairs committee encourages development of landscape design and architecture programs and courses.

Landscape Architect Network (LAN)
e-mail: office@landarchs.com
website: http://landarchs.com

As one of the few websites dedicated to landscape architects, LAN contains dozens of informative articles related to the field along with job listings, competitions, and book reviews.

Production Designer

A Few Facts

Number of Jobs
About 11,930 people working in production design in 2015

Salaries
The median wage for a production designer in 2015 was $54,920.

Educational Requirements
Bachelor's degree in fine arts, theater production, or set design

Personal Qualities
Creativity and the ability to draw, work with a team, use design software, and read blueprints

Work Settings
Offices, theaters, and soundstages

Future Job Outlook
Demand for production designers is predicted to grow by 9 percent through 2024, slightly higher than the average of 7 percent for all occupations.

What Does a Production Designer Do?

When you're watching a television show with people laughing in a restaurant, hurling through outer space, or running the country from the Oval Office, look past the actors on the screen. While the people may appear to be in an eatery, a spacecraft, or the White House, they are actually on a stage set. And almost every stage set has its origins in the creative mind of a production designer. Production designers are artists who combine drawings, paintings, architecture, and set decoration skills to create the entire physical surroundings in which a production takes place.

Production designers were once known in the film community as art directors. Today they are referred to as set designers, theatrical designers, or scenographers. Production designers are entertainment professionals who oversee the entire art department for a TV show, movie, play, opera, or dance performance. Production designers work with producers, directors, costume designers, and prop masters (employees who source or manufacture

Working with a Team

"Teamwork is the best aspect of my job. Ours is a real profession, with a contract, a project, a budget and deadlines. . . . We have to be ready to model our ideas based on necessity, to learn to study and understand the other professions we collaborate with: from light design, to literature, and music. In particular, we have to know how to work in an international team. You're collaborating with different professions and social extractions: from shoemakers to doormen, up to the orchestra director. It's fundamental to be able to dialogue with everyone, going from one language to another, literally and figuratively."

Lancia, "Designing Scenic Space: Interview with Set Designer Margherita Palli," March 29, 2013. www.lanciatrendvisions.com.

props). Some production designers decorate concert stages and backgrounds of photo and video shoots. The job of the production designer is to create and develop the overall look, atmosphere, and emotional feel of a story.

Production designers draw on a wide range of knowledge, talent, and skills to perform their jobs. They need to be artists who can sketch and paint drawings of set designs and backdrops. Production designers also need construction, drafting, and engineering skills. These abilities are used to produce plans for building scenery and for engineering scenery that changes positions in stage plays. Additionally, production designers need to prepare cost estimates for productions and manage budgets while sets are under construction. Production designer Gene Allen explained his job to the *New York Times*: "We're an odd lot certainly. More or less creative individuals trained in the visual arts and who, by the grace of the director, function as visual conceptualists—that is, translating the screenplay from a written document into pulsating . . . images."

Production designers rely on technical skills to work with computers and design software. Jen Chu, who has designed sets for shows on MTV, Bravo, and other networks, made note of this on the Design*Sponge website: "The single most important skill that I possess as a set designer is the ability to do basic 3D rendering and graphic design. Nowadays people expect to see digital sketches of everything, so you have to be able to visually convey your ideas to the client. At the very least, learn SketchUp and Photoshop." Other software used by production designers includes Vectorworks, Maya, Illustrator, and Rhino.

The most exciting—and difficult—task performed by a production designer is matching stage sets, costumes, and props to the script being performed. The hit play *Hamilton* takes place in eighteenth-century America; the TV show *The Walking Dead* is about a postapocalyptic world overrun by zombies; and the 2015 movie *Bridge of Spies* takes place in the early 1960s. In each case production designers oversaw the sets that provided a sense of realism to the production. Production designers often comb through old newspapers, books, and magazines to give authenticity to their sets. They might visit museums to view ancient paintings and statues. Science fiction novels and comic books provide inspiration for outer space and superhero productions.

Production designer Bill Groom worked on two hit shows set in the 1920s, *Downton Abbey* and *Boardwalk Empire*. In an article for the Deadline website, Groom eloquently explained his job: "We're trying to tell the story with objects—a light through the window, the furniture they have. It's said the poet sees the world in a doorknob . . . in such a small area, a poet can say so much. I think we are charged with something similar—we have a few moments in time to tell the story."

How to Become a Production Designer

Traditionally, Hollywood and Broadway production designers started as painters, carpenters, or stylists in scenery departments. Students who wish to gain this type of experience should work on school theater productions or volunteer for productions staged at community or college theaters. Prospective production designers can also find opportunities working with a studio photographer or a video production company. As Hollywood set designer Ken Larson writes on his educational blog, "Get professional experience in anything related. Anyone can, in time, produce a Set Design. Someone without skill might take years, but in time, they can do it."

Do You Need a College Degree?

It is possible to work your way up to a set designing career from within a production company, but in this highly competitive field formal schooling is a plus. A degree in fine arts, interior design, or performing arts will help you find work as a production designer. While obtaining their degrees students can get hands-on experience working in school theater productions or as interns.

Your Portfolio Is Your Job Ticket

As with most professions in the arts, a portfolio is necessary for anyone seeking employment as a production designer. But while a photographer or a web designer can inexpensively whip up a portfolio, production design hopefuls probably won't be building sample sets in their backyards to show prospective employers. But those seeking entry-level production design jobs can still assemble a portfolio using work done in school or community productions.

Prospective production designers should digitally scan their sketches and take photographs of sets, props, costumes, and anything else that can be assembled into an online portfolio. In addition, a business card and short résumé with a few photos can be thrust into the hands of a producer or director. In his blog Larson provides this insight about what to do once you've given someone your résumé: "Call them from time to time to remind them. People in this industry have very short memories. I can't tell you how many people said, 'Thank you. Your work was great. I'll call you the next time,' and I never hear from these people again."

A Day in the Life of a Production Designer

Overseeing the design and creation of costumes, backdrops, and props requires great imagination, stamina, determination, and adaptability from a production designer. Whether the work is in movies, theater, or on TV shows the tasks are many and the days are long; a typical production designer works twelve hours a day and, frequently, seven days a week.

It can take from three to eight weeks to build sets and props, depending on the production. Because of this time lag, the production designer is the first person a producer contacts when a script is finished and a project is approved to move forward. The production designer typically breaks the script down into all of the sets that are associated with the scenes. The next step requires research; a script might call for scenes in a restaurant, a lawyer's office, or a school for magicians.

Whatever scenes are called for, the production designer makes sketches of each set. After they are approved by the director, the production designer drafts blueprints for building plans. Sometimes scale models are made. The production designer chooses paint finishes, wall coverings, flooring, and anything else architecturally related. From that point the production designer works with carpenters, electricians, and painters to construct the set, and with film crews who conduct test shoots to see what the finished set looks like on camera. In an interview for ConnectEd Studios, production designer Denny Dugally, who worked on the TV show *Brothers and Sisters*, commented on her job, "I'm there for the entire process. This job can be extremely difficult. Every single day there are challenges that are thrown at me. It's hard, it's very stressful but it's so much fun."

Some production designers work on soundstages or studio sets, while others work on location. *On location* means filming in an actual setting rather than a soundstage or studio lot. For example, outdoor scenes that took place in the fictional town of Woodbury, Georgia, in *The Walking Dead* were actually filmed on location in the small town of Senoia, about 25 miles (40 km) south of Atlanta.

Sometimes production designers are required to oversee the

creation of a huge number of sets. When production designer Derek Hill worked on the 2013 miniseries *Bonnie & Clyde* (about two 1930s bank robbers) he was asked to build 189 sets in forty-two days: "Do you realize the math on that?" asks Hill. When Hill began he combed through old newsreels and newspaper clippings to accurately create scenes like banks and stores where Bonnie Parker and Clyde Barrow committed their crimes. Hill describes how he created the sets where the miniseries was filmed around Baton Rouge, Louisiana: "I found an old bar that was a general store at one time and we gutted it and built a set within that space. We found an abandoned sugar cane plantation warehouse that we gutted and made into a prison, and then, using photos from the Huntsville, Texas prison (where Barrow spent time), re-created the bunk room."

The Lowdown on a Career in Production Design

Because of the nature of show business, most production design work is temporary. Movies are usually produced over the course of a few months, while plays and TV shows can be canceled after a few years—or a few weeks. This means most production designers do not have full-time work over long periods of time.

Production design jobs do not come easily, but they do exist for those who are willing to seek them out and move to where the jobs are. According to the Bureau of Labor Statistics, the median wage for a production designer in 2015 was $54,920. That year the Art Directors Guild listed 330 members as set designers in Hollywood—and only 80 percent were employed. This means 20 percent of the skilled production designers were not working. Fortunately for production designers, there are opportunities for work outside Los Angeles. Many movies and TV shows are shot in Georgia, North Carolina, New Mexico, Seattle, Chicago, and Vancouver, Canada. Most film production companies hire local production designers in such cases.

For someone interested in art, architecture, style, and design working as a production designer can be a dream job. As Dugally said in her ConnectEd Studios interview, "It's almost a crime that I get paid for what I do. I love my job."

Find Out More

American Association of Community Theatre (AACT)
1300 Gendy St.
Fort Worth, TX 76107
phone: (866) 687-2228
website: www.aact.org

The AACT is the national community theater organization whose chief goal is to enable community theaters across the country to provide quality entertainment, intellectual stimulation, and opportunities for theater workers.

Art Directors Guild (ADG)
11969 Ventura Blvd., 2nd Floor
Studio City, CA 91604
phone: (818) 762-9995
website: www.adg.org

The ADG is a union comprised of art directors, graphic artists, illustrators, model makers, production designers, scenic artists, and set designers.

Wingspace Theatrical Design
232 Third St. #C301
Brooklyn, NY 11215
website: http://wingspace.com

Wingspace is a collective of designers whose mission is to promote collaboration in the field of theatrical design while fostering a larger conversation about design, its principles, and the cooperative spirit within the community.

Music Therapist

A Few Facts

Number of Jobs

Approximately 10,000 people were employed as music therapists in 2015.

Salaries

The average annual salary is about $48,066.

Educational Requirements

Bachelor's degree or higher in music therapy

Personal Qualities

Music and singing abilities, sense of humor and empathy, an interest in people, a desire to help others

Work Settings

Indoors in hospitals, day-care centers, nursing homes, and hospices

Future Job Outlook

The demand for music therapists is expected to grow by 12 percent through 2024, faster than average for all occupations.

What Does a Music Therapist Do?

Music therapy was in the news in 2015 when ABC's *World News Tonight* named "all music therapists" as "Persons of the Week." The accompanying news story featured Houston music therapist Meaghan Morrow and described the important role that music therapists play in helping people with brain injuries. Morrow worked with Arizona congresswoman Gabrielle Giffords after she was shot in the head by a crazed gunman in Tucson in 2011. Giffords survived but suffered from aphasia—the inability to speak because of damage to the language pathways in her brain's left hemisphere. However, after working with Morrow for several months Giffords regained her ability to speak. "Nothing activates the brain so extensively as music," Dr. Oliver Sacks, professor of neurology at Columbia University, told ABC News. "People who have lost speech, may sing."

Giffords's case attracted widespread attention but music therapists accomplish similar wonders every day working with Alzheimer's patients, wounded veterans, and developmentally disabled children and adults. When patients sing, drum, or participate in a musical performance with music therapists the shared experience helps reduce feelings of isolation. Music therapy helps release repressed emotions and reduces anxiety and depression. Music therapy has also been shown to calm people by slowing their breath rate and heartbeat and by lowering blood pressure and even body temperature.

Music therapists use music as part of an overall rehabilitation program, working in tandem with doctors, nurses, counselors, and speech and physical therapists. Music therapy is effective with those who have difficulty expressing themselves, such as children who have experienced severe trauma. Music therapists work with the elderly in nursing homes to improve physical, mental, and emotional functioning. Those who specialize in music therapy help people with mental disorders, substance abuse problems, and chronic pain. In addition, music therapy is used in hospitals to promote physical rehabilitation, to induce sleep, to counteract fear and elevate a patient's mood before and after surgery, and even to reduce stress during childbirth.

Personal qualifications for music therapists include the desire to help others, the capacity to adjust to changing conditions, and the ability to provide emotional support to clients and families. Music therapists need to be tactful, imaginative, and exhibit a sense of humor in sometimes trying circumstances. Flexibility is required in the workplace as clients can get frustrated or angry and might be prone to outbursts.

How to Become a Music Therapist

Above all else, music therapists need to be, well, musical. Most play guitar, keyboards, and sing. Many are also practiced in the use of rhythm instruments such as drums, tambourines, and maracas. They play recorded music for patients and know how to provide lessons and improvise and write songs. Some therapists work or have worked as entertainers. They know popular songs

A music therapist, on guitar, works with a client who taps out a rhythm on bongo drums. Music therapists work with nursing home residents, people with mental disorders, trauma victims, and others to counteract fear, elevate mood, and improve overall physical, mental, and emotional function.

that patients love and can sing along to. For example, Giffords's therapy involved her singing several personal favorites including "Maybe" from the Broadway musical *Annie* and the 1967 hit "Brown Eyed Girl" by Van Morrison. Other patients respond to rhythmic music like reggae or calypso because of the energizing, irresistible beats.

Do You Need a College Degree?

For students who live and breathe music but know in their heart of hearts that they cannot make a living as professional musicians, music therapy offers a happy compromise. It satisfies the desire to make music while at the same time sharing it with those who can truly appreciate it. But a love of music alone is not enough to get started in this profession. It requires a bachelor's degree in music therapy. Curriculum includes coursework in music, music therapy, biology, psychology, and social and behavioral sciences.

After college, music therapists are required to perform twelve hundred hours of fieldwork as interns in health care or educational facilities. During this time therapists learn to analyze the needs of clients and develop and implement treatment plans. Once the clinical training is complete, music therapists obtain official credentials by passing an examination administered by the accredited Certification Board for Music Therapists. Passing will give the music therapist the designation of Music Therapist-Board Certified (MT-BC). Therapists need to retake the exam every five years. A music therapist who goes by the name Kalani offers this advice on the Careers in Music website: "It's not a fallback career. Lots of people don't make it through [the degree program]. It's lots of work, but it's rewarding. Don't take it lightly."

Working as a Music Therapist

Music therapists work in many settings, including general and psychiatric hospitals, physical rehabilitation centers, nursing homes, schools, prisons, substance abuse programs, day-care centers, and hospices. Some work a forty- to fifty-hour workweek, while others prefer part-time work. Freelance music therapists develop contacts with health care or social service agencies and work for hourly rates or contractual fees.

Like any therapist, a music therapist's daily work is focused on the client. In some cases therapists work with groups of patients. Before starting therapy with any client the music therapist assesses the patient's needs and desires and identifies goals and objectives. This enables the music therapist to develop a treatment program.

Music therapists work with a wide range of clients throughout the day. A therapist might conduct group therapy with children with autism from 10:00 to 10:30 a.m., work with developmentally disabled children until 11 a.m., and conduct therapy with individual patients until lunch. The afternoon might begin with a meeting attended by doctors and other therapists to discuss ongoing therapy programs. A therapist might also spend time planning and rehearsing for upcoming musical performances given by clients on holidays such as Halloween, Christmas, and Thanksgiving. And many music therapists spend one or two days a week supervising music therapy interns who are working to obtain their degrees.

Elizabeth Huss is among the growing number of music therapists who operate private practices. In an interview with the Performing Arts Schools website, Huss said she drives from place to place to provide hour-long sessions for clients with a wide range of problems: "I work with children with severe emotional disturbance and also some with developmental handicaps. . . . Some of these kids have been abused, some have bipolar disorder, some have schizophrenia, quite a few have ADHD, some are autistic, cerebral palsy—all different kinds." Huss tailors therapy for specific ailments. Her daily work involves teaching children to express themselves through drumming and making up silly songs to improve their speech patterns. Huss even allows kids to pound tunelessly on a piano to take out their frustrations.

Some music therapists specialize in working with the elderly who often find relief from respiratory problems by singing. Alzheimer's patients also connect to the outside world through song; even

Changing the Mood in an Alzheimer's Unit

"I did a rhythm exercise with a group of patients on an Alzheimer's unit. . . . There were people who were very agitated and wouldn't respond to much at all, there were people who were falling asleep, and there were people who were very active. A huge range. I brought out some drums and we played along with a song. I saw changes in every single person's level of involvement. The agitated people calmed down, the non-responders started tapping their fingers, the person who would previously only interact with me turned and began to interact with someone else in the group."

Jack Sibley, "Interview with Music Therapist, Elizabeth Huss," Performing Arts Schools, 2012. http://performingartsschools.com.

Improving Communication and Social Skills

"I leave my house at 10:00 a.m. and drive to a school to work with a 12-year old student who is visually impaired, uses a wheelchair, and is nonverbal. I use neurologic music therapy interventions to help facilitate reaching and locating sounds, making choices, and improving sensory integration. . . . After a 50-minute session I return to my car to drive to another school where I provide 30-minute music therapy groups to four classrooms of children aged 3-18, diagnosed with autism. The music therapy group sessions are designed to work on communication, motor coordination, and social skills through drumming, singing, songwriting, and moving with music."

Berklee, "Alumni Interview with Dr. Krystal Demaine," 2016. www.berklee.edu.

those who cannot speak will sometimes sing, hum along, or at least react in a positive manner. A music therapist might play multiple songs to someone with severe dementia until the patient responds to a single tune. That will become the patient's contact song, one the therapist plays at every session. In an interview with Caring.com, musical therapist Concetta Tomaino describes working with two of her clients: "I knew that when I played [contact songs], Mary or Sarah would open her eyes, look at me, and start to smile. . . . The more their attention was engaged . . . the more other pieces of their behavior and their personality started coming out."

Music therapists also work with stroke patients who have lost the ability to walk and are trying to relearn those motions. Trying to make the physical body obey the mind can be extremely frustrating for these patients. A music therapist would approach this challenge with drums or rhythmic music. As Tomaino told Caring.com, "the rhythm provides the structure within which they move. And because they're following the music, they're not thinking about lifting each leg individually. It's almost as if they're using past memories of how to move with music."

Making a Connection

A music therapist's workday can be difficult; a therapist builds emotional relationships with clients who are sick and suffering. Molly Hicks works with hospice patients who have terminal diseases and don't have long to live. However, Hicks emphasizes that while her patients do eventually die many live for quite a while. Her job is to focus on helping them find meaning in their lives and help them to die as painlessly and free from anxiety as possible. In an interview on First Day Press, Hicks said: "[The] hospice is about enhancing quality of *life* for as long as possible, during a period in which individual moments in time become more precious."

The music therapist and client establish a unique bond based on music—and this can be especially rewarding for both. On the Performing Arts Schools website, Elizabeth Huss described a patient who had severe cognitive disabilities; she did not respond at all to speech or touch. Huss picks up the story: "But once you start playing the music she'll start smiling and shaking her head to the beat of the music. Just having that connection—bringing her out of herself—is amazing."

The Lowdown on a Career as a Music Therapist

The American Music Therapy Association says the average annual salary of music therapists is $48,066. The field is expected to grow at a 12 percent rate through 2024. According to the Bureau of Labor Statistics, as the large baby-boomer population ages, music therapists will be in demand to treat age-related injuries and illnesses.

While becoming a music therapist might sound like a good career move for a musician who wants to strum the guitar all day, it is not a job for everyone. It requires long hours of study, intern work, and passing certification exams. As Kalani told Careers in Music, a love for music is secondary: "Your number one goal has to be to help people."

Music therapists say their biggest challenge is a lack of awareness about their field. A new graduate might struggle to find work in parts of the country where the benefits of music therapy are not well understood. This means most full-time music therapy jobs are in large metropolitan areas. Therapists living outside cities often have to set up their own practices and sell their services to health care providers and others. Once doctors and hospital administrators understand the benefits of music therapy, however, plenty of work usually follows.

Find Out More

American Music Therapy Association (AMTA)
8455 Colesville Rd., Suite 1000
Silver Spring, MD 20910
phone: (301) 589-3300
website: www.musictherapy.org

The AMTA supports the therapeutic use of music in rehabilitation, special education, and community settings and is committed to the advancement of education, training, professional standards, credentials, and research in support of the music therapy profession.

Voices
PO Box 7810
NO-5020 Bergen
Norway
phone: 47.97.11.9246

Voices promotes music therapy as a global enterprise and encourages the growth of music therapy in developing countries.

World Federation of Music Therapy (WFMT)
website: www.wfmt.info

The WFMT is an international nonprofit organization bringing together music therapy associations, individuals, and students interested in developing and promoting music therapy globally.

Game Designer

A Few Facts

Number of Jobs

Estimated 212,510 video game designers in the United States

Salaries

Average salary of $75,065 in 2015

Educational Requirements

Bachelor's degree in game design, software engineering, film, computer graphics, or mathematics

Personal Qualities

Creative vision, patience, detail oriented, able to work with a team

Work Settings

Indoors, in offices and studios.

Future Job Outlook

Expected to grow by about 6 percent through 2022

What Does a Game Designer Do?

More than 1.2 billion people—or one out of every six people on Earth—played video games in 2015. In the United States 155 million people—nearly half the population—plays video games regularly. These numbers show that video games are deeply rooted in modern culture. And video game designers are at the center of this social phenomenon. Writing in a video game industry brochure, Michael D. Gallagher, CEO of the Entertainment Software Association, calls video game designers "some of the most innovative minds in the tech sector." Video game designers, he writes, "continue to push the entertainment envelope."

Video game designers visualize and implement video game mechanics, animation, characters, narrative, artwork, artificial intelligence (AI) behavior, text, and sound. Designers combine their game-playing enthusiasm with the skills necessary to create products that are exciting, entertaining, and artistic. Video games consist of millions of lines of computer code and video game designers must be masters of computer software. They write code to generate commands, events, scenes, functions, and objects that are part of the gameplay. Game designers are obsessed with detail and can spot mistakes even in games designed to confound expert players. Since new game designs have numerous bugs and potential problems the craft requires a perfectionist who has laser-sharp focus—and a degree of patience rarely required in other tech fields.

Video game designers are team players. They work in groups to create video games in their many forms from simple apps to immersive virtual reality games. A video game designer's team includes production people who create basic game concepts, decide on the game's target audience, and devise schedules and budgets.

Bringing Game Worlds to Life

Video game designers often specialize in a single aspect of game production. Content designers work on games before they are produced, creating a game's overall plot, characters, and settings. While content designers can let their imaginations run wild they must stick to cohesive themes. For example, if a game takes place in medieval times, the content designer must be sure not to include things that might not be of the era, such as a pistol or a Roman chariot.

Game mechanics designers focus on the rules of a game and what is called the balance or fairness of the game. As game designer Mark Newheiser explains on the Strange Horizons website, "fairness can either mean that everyone has a chance [to win], or that winning is entirely a result of skill."

Those who work as level designers are also called environmental designers. They design fantasy or realistic environments and create characters and objects that inhabit each playing level of the game. Environmental designer Caleb Parrish, who has worked on multiple games in the *Spiderman* and *Assassin's Creed* series, explained his work in an interview with the Games

Keep It Simple at the Start

"When the three of us feel good about any particular idea, we start developing a prototype with basic colored shapes to show to friends, family, and even strangers. We can get a sense for just how fun our core game mechanic can be without fancy art and music clouding the user's judgment. Showing the game to everyone who will listen and quickly . . . [changing it] based on their feedback is how we know when we want to take an idea to the next level. There's a fine line there though. We're always careful not to take every piece of feedback to heart."

Matt Spiel, "Interview: Game Designer—Jake Fleming," *Treehouse* (blog), July 7, 2014. http://blog.teamtreehouse.com.

Industry Career Guide: "I get the chance to bring game worlds to life. Sometimes it's taking a blueprint or even a 3D model from a designer and fleshing it out into an immersive, believable place. Sometimes it's from scratch, where I just need to make something that looks cool."

Some game designers specialize in artificial intelligence, dictating how computer-controlled opponents and allies react strategically and realistically to a player's moves. Kris Graft, editor in chief of the Gamasutra website, blogs about the importance of AI in gaming: "Artificial intelligence in video games helps bring virtual worlds to life; it lurks beneath the surface, determining the way a player interacts with a game. As the brains of a game, AI engages our brains."

Lead game designers are in charge of the entire operation. They take sketches and ideas from brainstorming sessions and turn them into video games. They create concise documentation for every aspect of the game, including locations, characters, rules, objects, and playing modes. The lead designer coordinates with artists, programmers, and other design staff. After each person has been assigned their specific tasks, the lead game designer ensures that the game designs are properly implemented and that development is on schedule and within budget.

The Look and Feel of the Game

Video game artists are specialists who work in the video game design field and use their artistic skills and technical knowledge to provide the look and feel of games. Video game artists create all the artwork for environments, characters, objects, and other visual elements. Video game artists often use traditional artistic skills such as drawing, painting, and sculpting to create models. The original artwork is then digitized with advanced 3D modeling and other software programs. When the artwork is completed, video game artists use their knowledge of advanced mathematics and complex algorithms to bring the artwork of the game to the screen.

Although video game artists represent one specialty of game design, individuals in this group tend to focus their talents on particular areas. Concept artists, for instance, produce hundreds of scenes, structures, key moments, and storyboards which guide the overall look of a game. Modelers build 3D characters and environments on digital frames, based on the concept art. Motion-capture artists record the movements of real people and objects which are digitized by modelers. Audio artists develop, record, and process all of a game's sounds, including music, dialogue, and game noises; they also work with audio engineers, composers, voice actors, and musicians.

How to Become a Game Designer

If you want to become a video game designer you must have an all-consuming passion for playing video games. Playing provides experience with games and allows you to absorb how games are structured while providing inspiration for you to design your own games. You need to have some drawing ability and a solid knowledge of graphic design, 3D modeling, and animation software, including Autodesk 3ds Max and Maya. Video game designers usually have computer programming skills and are familiar with Python, Perl, and C++ coding languages. Excellent written and verbal communication skills are absolutely necessary. Prospective game designers also need to remain up to date on popular trends in gaming and the gaming industry.

One of the most important aptitudes is attitude; game designers need to work cooperatively with others. As Ben Bell, producer of *The Sims 3: Pets*, told *Occupational Outlook Quarterly*: "Successful work on a collaborative project is something we look for in hiring new employees." Parrish puts it another way on the Games Industry Career Guide. He says the least favorite part of his job is egotistical team members. "Nothing kills a team dynamic like a prima-donna and nothing muddies up the creative process like someone refusing to put the goals of the project before their own."

Most large video game producers require, or strongly prefer, game designers to hold a bachelor's degree in game design, software engineering, or related programs. Game design courses cover drawing, scripting, 2D and 3D modeling, animation, level and interface design, and storyboard rendering.

A Day in the Life of a Game Designer

Most video game designers will say there is no such thing as a typical workday. The tasks that are completed depend on the product the designer is working on, the size of the team, and what phase the project is in. For example, when a new game is proposed the day begins with a brainstorming session where designers pitch ideas for various aspects of the game while artists make sketches and storyboards. When a project is in production, there will be long hours of work building a game with computer code. This work is interspersed with meetings with other game designers, engineers, and product managers; changes are discussed and schedules are updated. When projects are nearing completion, workers test games and attune game attributes, all the while bearing down to complete a project in time. In an interview with Econsultancy, Pete Low, who is a game designer at a

Start Now Designing Your Own Games

"You need to know what can actually be made in a game if you want to design one or solve a problem that arises. You can start becoming a designer now, actually! Design games on your own, even if they're card games or board games, it's almost all the same process. Generate ideas and practice writing them all out as though you were going to hand your written game pitch to a programmer and they were going to make it based off what you wrote. Attend local game jams and hone your skills now because every game you attempt to make will bring you a big step closer to achieving your dream."

Kat Shanahan, "Get to Know a Game Designer: An Interview with Abby Friesen," *Inside Filament* (blog), September 28, 2015. www.filamentgames.com.

digital content company called Chunk, explained: "There are a wide range of skills involved with game design and you may be asked to call upon all of them in a single day."

But as strange as it might seem, working on video games all day is not always fun. Video game designers are often under intense pressure to produce with limited time and resources. Designers, artists, and programmers often labor long hours for months at a time when faced with looming deadlines. In addition the video game industry is extremely competitive and the pressure to succeed is intense. A bad video game, or one that is not well received, can spell financial trouble for a studio and its designers. This can cause incredible stress as David Sirlin, lead designer for Sirlin Games, explains in *Occupational Outlook Quarterly*: "We are trying to catch lightning in a bottle. It can be soul crushing when you find out that your game really doesn't work."

The Lowdown on a Career as a Game Designer

Working as a video game designer might seem like a dream come true to someone who spends most of their waking hours playing video games. And there are plenty of advantages to working in the video game industry, especially when it comes to earnings. While the Bureau of Labor Statistics does not collect data specific to video game workers, various online surveys show that entry-level annual salaries for video game designers start at around $45,000. Designers with three years in the industry can expect to earn around $83,410 a year. Video game artists earned an average of at least $68,000, while programmers averaged more than $85,000. Top-level video game designers earn nearly $127,000.

Find Out More

Academy of Interactive Arts & Sciences (AIAS)
11175 Santa Monica Blvd., 4th Floor
Los Angeles, CA 90025
phone: (310) 484-2560
website: www.interactive.org

The AIAS was founded in 1996 to recognize outstanding achievements in interactive entertainment. The organization has several scholarship programs to support students who are pursuing careers in interactive entertainment.

Entertainment Software Association (ESA)
575 Seventh St. NW, Suite 300
Washington, DC 20004
e-mail: esa@theesa.com
website: www.theesa.com

An association dedicated to serving the needs of companies that publish computer and video games, the ESA maintains a list of US colleges and universities offering video game courses and degrees.

International Game Developers Association (IGDA)

19 Mantua Rd.
Mt. Royal, NJ 08061
e-mail: robert@stridepr.com
website: www.igda.org

The IGDA is the largest nonprofit membership organization serving individuals who create video games. The organization cultivates opportunities for video game designers and helps them advance in the profession.

Video Game Development Association (VGDA)

1250 N. Bellflower Blvd.
Long Beach, CA 90840
website: www.vgda.net

The mission of the VGDA is to utilize game development as a platform to expand and enhance the professional and personal lives of its members and to advocate for game development in the educational, social, and political realms.

Interview with a
Landscape Designer

Carol Armour Aronson is a landscape designer in Los Angeles, California. She has worked as a landscape designer for five years. She spoke to the author by phone about her career.

Q: Why did you become a landscape designer?

A: I love plants and I like to be outside. I also care about maintaining suitable islands of native habitat in cities to support indigenous wildlife. I live in California where the ornamental plants you see in many yards were originally brought here from other places like Africa, South America, and Australia. These plants are beautiful but they don't support local wildlife whereas native plants have evolved with native insects and local bird populations.

Q: Can you describe your training?

A: I took fifteen hundred hours of landscape certification classes at an adult education institution. I learned plant identification, pruning, landscape design, soils, tools, and hardscaping, which refers to sidewalks, walls, ponds, and other features. I did hands-on training, using power tools like motorized trimmers and Dingo earthmovers. After becoming certified I got a scholarship in an associate's degree program for horticulture with an emphasis on landscape design.

Q: Can you describe your typical workday?

A: No day is typical, that is what I most enjoy about my job. Some days I spend with clients finding out what they like and want. Other days I'm measuring and taking pictures of the site, or digging up soil samples. Still other days are spent drawing a base plan, researching plants and creating a design. I spend days visiting nurseries to buy plants, and visiting botanical gardens and hiking to see plants in their mature stages. When I'm involved in installation work I drive around and pick up parts, manage landscape workers, and sometimes roll up my sleeves and perform some of the labor.

Q: Do you have a special license?

A: In California landscape designers do not need a special license for design but they do need a contractor's license to do installation work over $600. That amount only covers a few plants and trees. While most landscape designers don't do installation, I also have a landscape contractor's license to do installation which involves paths, patios, planting, and allows me to do commercial projects.

Q: What do you like most about your job?

A: I love the daily variety and the challenge of creating something beautiful.

Q: What do you like least?

A: When I lose control over a project. Sometimes the installer or the client changes my design without understanding the long-term ramifications of the new plants or the location they have selected to change.

Q: What personal qualities do you find most valuable for this type of work?

A: Being able to work independently, listening to the client's needs and wants, and being thorough on my research. The most important thing is to trust my design instincts!

Q: What advice do you have for students who might be interested in this career?

A: Get to know your native plants, soils, wildlife, and insects. Know your type of climate and what plants do best in which locations. Treat each project as its own microclimate. Be a people person!

Q: Can you describe something about your job that is especially rewarding?

A: Having someone tell me they get joy every day out of my landscape creation. And awards; one of my designs received a Beautiful Gardens award from the city of La Cañada Flintridge in 2016.

Q: How important are artistic abilities to your career?

A: Artistic abilities are very important to me since I sketch my designs by hand. I do base plans on regular paper then use tracing paper over the base plan so I make changes as I go along. I work with pencils, an architect's scale, and Prismacolor markers, which you can blend. That said, there are many computer programs that do beautiful professional layouts.

Q: What would you say is the biggest challenge you have faced in your job?

A: The biggest challenge is making sure the client spends the money to install appropriate irrigation systems for their new landscape. If they water by hand, most overwater their plants. So if I leave them with manual irrigation they water too much or at the wrong time of day when it's too hot. When plants are babies they need more water; when they are older they need less.

Other Careers If You Like the Arts

Actor
Announcer
Architect
Art director
Art historian
Art therapist
Buyer and purchasing agent
Cartoonist
Choreographer
Comic book artist
Craft artist
Dancer
Desktop publisher
Drafter
Fine artist
Floral designer
Hair stylist
Industrial designer
Interior designer
Jeweler, precious stone, and
    metalworker
Jewelry designer

Lithographer
Makeup artist
Medical illustrator
Model
Museum curator
Music composer
Musician and singer
Music teacher
Nail artist
Package designer
Producer and director
Product designer
Reporter
Screen printer
Sound engineering technician
Tattoo artist
Textile designer
Theater director
Transportation designer
Video game director
Web developer
Writer

Editor's note: The online *Occupational Outlook Handbook* of the US Department of Labor's Bureau of Labor Statistics is an excellent source of information on jobs in hundreds of career fields, including many of those listed here. The *Occupational Outlook Handbook* may be accessed online at www.bls.gov/ooh.

Academy of Interactive Arts &
Sciences (AIAS), 22–23, 73
Acme Filmworks, 20
Adobe Creative Suite, 9
AIGA, 14, 23
Alzheimer's patients, 63–64
American Association of
Community Theatre (AACT), 57
American Music Therapy
Association (AMTA), 66
American Society of Landscape
Architects (ASLA), 49
American Society of Media
Photographers (ASMP), 40
animators, 5, 16–24
best cities for, 20–22
career preparation for, 17–18
educational requirements for,
16, 18
job outlook for, 16, 22
overview of, 16–17
portfolios of, 18–19
resources for, 22–24
salaries of, 16, 22
Aronson, Carol Armour, 75–77
art and design schools, 22
Art Career Project, 23
art careers, 4
benefits and rewards of, 6
fashion designers and, 25–32
game designers and, 67–74
graphic designers and, 7–15
landscape designers and, 42–50
multimedia artists and animators
and, 16–24
music therapists and, 59–66
and other careers, 78
photographers and, 33–41
production designers and,
51–58
art directors, 12, 14, 51
Art Directors Guild (ADG), 57–58
artificial intelligence, 69
artistic style, 17
arts
freelance opportunities in the,
4–5
majors in the, 4
role of the, 4
ASIFA-Hollywood, 23
associate's degree, 11
Association of International
Photography Art Dealers
(AIPAD), 40
Association of Professional
Landscape Designers (APLD),
49–50
audio artists, 70

bachelor's degree
See also educational
requirements
for fashion designers, 28
for game designers, 71
for graphic designers, 10–11
for landscape designers, 46
for multimedia artists and
animators, 18

for music therapists, 61
Bell, Ben, 71
Bureau of Labor Statistics (BLS),
5, 14, 16, 49, 57, 73
Business of Fashion (BOF), 31

California, 20–21, 22
career advancement, for graphic
designer, 12–13
career preparation
for fashion designers, 27
for game designers, 70–71, 72
for graphic designers, 8–10
for landscape designers, 44–45
for multimedia artists and
animators, 17–18
for music therapists, 60–61
for photographers, 35–36
for production designers, 53–54
Cartoon Network, 20
Certification Board for Music
Therapists, 62
certifications, for music therapists,
62
Chanel, Coco, 26
Chu, Jen, 52–53
clothing industry, 26
college degrees. See associate's
degree; bachelor's degree;
educational requirements
Color Marketing Group (CMG), 15
computer-aided design (CAD)
software, 30
computer-generated images, 17
computer programming skills, 71
concept artists, 70
content designers, 68
creativity, 27, 33, 46

dailies, 20
design schools, 22
design skills, 8–9
design software, 8–9, 52–53
drawing skills, 17, 27
DreamWorks, 21
Dugally, Denny, 55, 57

EA Games, 21
Eastman, George, 33
educational requirements
for fashion designers, 25, 28
for game designers, 67, 71
for graphic designers, 7, 10–11
for landscape designers, 42, 46
for multimedia artists and
animators, 16, 18
for music therapists, 59, 61–62
for photographers, 33, 35–36
for production designers, 51, 54
employment growth, 5, 22
employment opportunities
freelance, 4–5
See also job outlook
entertainment industry, 6, 21–22
Entertainment Software
Association (ESA), 73
event photographers, 34–35
expertise, development of, 8

Facebook, 38, 39
fashion designers, 6, 25–32
career preparation for, 27
educational requirements for,
25, 28
job outlook for, 25, 31
overview of, 25–27
portfolios of, 28–30
resources for, 31–32
salaries of, 25, 31
typical workday for, 25, 30–31
fashion photographers, 34
fashion shows, 31
Fashion Weeks, 31
Fleming, Jake, 69
forensic photographers, 34, 36
Fox TV Animation, 20
freelance opportunities, 4–5,
13–14, 30, 62
Freelancers Union, 5

Gallagher, Michael D., 67
game designers, 6, 18, 67–74
career preparation for, 70–71, 72
educational requirements for,
67, 71
job outlook for, 67
number of jobs for, 67
overview of, 67–68
resources for, 73–74
salaries of, 67, 73
specialties, 68–70
typical workday for, 69, 71–72
work settings for, 67
game mechanics designers, 68
Giffords, Gabrielle, 59, 61
Gladwell, Malcolm, 8
Graphic Artists Guild, Inc., 24
graphic designers, 7–15
career advancement for, 12–13
career preparation for, 8–10
educational requirements for,
7, 10–11
job outlook for, 7, 14
overview of, 7–8
portfolios of, 11–12
qualities of, 13
resources for, 14–15
salaries of, 7, 14
typical workday for, 7, 12
Groening, Matt, 4
Groom, Bill, 53

haute couture, 30
Hill, Derek, 56
Hollywood, 6
humility, 12–13
Hurley, Peter, 39

image editing software, 34
imagination, 4
inner artist, 6
International Federation of
Landscape Architects (IFLA), 50
International Game Developers
Association (IGDA), 74
internships, for music therapists,

61–62
Ive, Jonathan, 4

job outlook
  for fashion designers, 25, 31
  for game designers, 67
  for graphic designers, 7, 14
  for landscape designers, 42, 49
  for multimedia artists and
    animators, 16, 22
  for music therapists, 59, 65–66
  for photographers, 33, 39
  for production designers, 51,
    56–57

Karan, Donna, 26
Klum, Heidi, 25–26
Kodak, 33
Kors, Michael, 26, 27

Lambton, Chris, 42–43
Landscape Architect Network
  (LAN), 50
landscape architects, 44
landscape designers, 6, 42–50
  career preparation for, 44–45
  educational requirements for,
    42, 46
  interview with, 75–77
  job outlook for, 42, 49
  overview of, 42–44
  portfolios for, 46–47
  resources for, 49–50
  rewards and challenges for, 77
  salaries of, 42, 49
  typical workday for, 47–49,
    75–76
  use of social media by, 42, 47
landscape design software, 47–48
Lauren, Ralph, 4, 26
Leibovitz, Annie, 4
level designers, 68–69
licenses, for landscape designers,
  76
Light & Magic, 21
look books, 29
Lucas, George, 21

MacFarlane, Seth, 20
micrographs, 35
microscopic photographers, 35
Monet, Claude, 44–45
Morrow, Meaghan, 59
motion-capture artists, 70
motion capture data (mocap), 17
multimedia artists, 6, 16–24
  career preparation for, 17–18
  educational requirements for,
    16, 18
  job outlook for, 16, 22
  number of jobs for, 16
  overview of, 16–17
  portfolios of, 18–19
  resources for, 22–24
  salaries of, 16, 22
  typical workday for, 19–20,
    62–63
multimedia software, 17
Music Therapist-Board Certified
  (MT-BC), 62
music therapists, 6, 59–66
  career preparation for, 60–61
  educational requirements for,
    59, 61–62
  job outlook for, 59, 65–66
  overview of, 59–60
  resources for, 66
  salaries of, 59, 65
  work settings for, 59, 62–64
music therapy, 59–60

National Press Photographers
  Association (NPPA), 40
nature photographers, 34, 37–38
New York City, 21–22
New York Fashion Week, 31
Nickelodeon, 22

Ogilvy & Mather, 21
O'Neill, Luke, 29–30
on location filming, 55
outdoor design software, 43

Padgett, Lance, 5
Parker, Trey, 20
Parrish, Caleb, 68–69, 71
Parsons, 22, 28
Pendergrass, Kimberly, 8, 10, 13
photographers, 33–41
  career preparation for, 35–36
  educational requirements for,
    33, 35–36
  job outlook for, 33, 39
  number of jobs for, 33
  overview of, 33–34
  portfolios of, 36–37
  resources for, 40–41
  salaries of, 33, 39
  self-employed, 34, 35
  typical workday for, 33, 37–38
  use of social media by, 38–39
photography, 33
photojournalists, 33, 34, 36
Picasso, Pablo, 6
Pixar Animation Studios, 21
Pixar University, 20
plagiarism, 10
portfolios
  fashion designer, 28–30
  graphic designer, 11–12
  landscape designer, 46–47
  multimedia artist and animator,
    18–19
  photographer, 36–37
  production designer, 54
production designers, 51–58
  career preparation for, 53–54
  educational requirements for,
    51, 54
  job outlook for, 51, 56–57
  overview of, 51–53
  portfolios for, 54
  resources for, 57–58
  salaries of, 51, 57
  skills needed by, 52–53
  typical workday for, 51, 55–56
Professional Photographers of
  America (PPA), 41
Project Runway, 25–26
prototypes, 69

Randall, Bonnie Baglioli, 18
Renegade Animation, 20
resources
  for fashion designers, 31–32
  for game designers, 73–74
  for graphic designer, 14–15
  for landscape designers, 49–50
  for multimedia artists and
    animators, 22–24
  for music therapists, 66
  for photographers, 40–41
  for production designers, 57–58
Rosenzweig, Gregg, 43

Sacks, Olivor, 59
Sagmeister, Stefan, 8
salaries
  fashion designer, 25, 31
  game designer, 67, 73

graphic designer, 7, 14
landscape designer, 42, 49
multimedia artist and animator,
  16, 22
music therapist, 59, 65
photographer, 33, 39
production designer, 51, 57
Sartore, Joel, 37–38
scenographers. See production
  designers
School of Visual Arts (SVA), 22
Schwab, Brian, 17–18, 21
self-employment, 34, 35, 47
  See also freelance opportunities
set designers. See production
  designers
sewing skills, 27
Silicon Valley, 6
Simpson, Charlotte, 26
Sirlin, David, 72
sketchbooks, 18
social media, 38–39, 47
social skills, 64
Society for Experiential Graphic
  Design (SEGD), 15
Society for Photographic
  Education (SPE), 41
software
  3D modeling, 70
  CAD, 30
  design, 8–9, 52–53
  image editing, 34
  landscape design, 47–48
  multimedia, 17
  outdoor design, 43
Spiel, Matt, 69
Stephenson, Jim, 37
Stern, Nick, 34–35
storyboards, 19
stroke patients, 64
StyleCareers, 32

theatrical designers. See
  production designers
3D modeling software, 70
Tisch School of the Arts, 22

University & College Designers
  Association (UCDA), 15
Upwork, 5

Viacom, 22
video game artists, 70, 73
Video Game Development
  Association (VGDA), 74
video games, 67–68
Vogue, 32
Voices, 66

Walt Disney Company, 20
web graphics designer, 14
Weiland, Craig, 8, 10, 13
wildlife photographers, 37–38
Wingspace Theatrical Design, 58
Women's Wear Daily, 32
workday, typical
  for fashion designers, 30–31
  for game designers, 71–72
  for graphic designers, 12
  for landscape designers, 47–49,
    75–76
  for multimedia artists and
    animators, 19–20
  for music therapists, 62–63
  for photographers, 37–38
  for production designers, 55–56
World Federation of Music Therapy
  (WFMT), 66

YouTube, 38–39